Ethical Standards in Forensic Science

Ethical Standards in Forensic Science

Harold Franck and Darren Franck

CRC Press
Taylor & Francis Group
Boca Raton London New York

CRC Press is an imprint of the
Taylor & Francis Group, an **informa** business

CRC Press
Taylor & Francis Group
6000 Broken Sound Parkway NW, Suite 300
Boca Raton, FL 33487-2742

International Standard Book Number-13: 978-1-138-49615-6 (Hardback)

Visit the Taylor & Francis Web site at
http://www.taylorandfrancis.com

and the CRC Press Web site at
http://www.crcpress.com

Contents

Foreword

By way of introduction, we wish to discuss a cautionary tale of how well-meaning intentions and an incorrect hypothesis can become interwoven into the fabric of ethical standards in forensic investigations. This tale does not imply that ethical standards were or have been compromised because such standards are moot with respect to the tale. We wish to use the tale to simply delineate facts from conjectures and show what science and engineering can prove or disprove. It also indicates that some facts cannot be conclusively proven at all times and in all instances. Rather, it is an example of how intense assertions or misguided or unproven beliefs can cloud judgment leading to incorrect beliefs or conclusions. In a strict sense, what we wish to describe is not a forensic engineering ethical failure, although it involves forensic engineering. The story involves documented events, witness statements, physical evidence, conjectures, unproven claims, and some sophisticated engineering conducted by the leading laboratory in explosions in the United States. Hopefully, this account will help set the stage for the theme of the book relative to the adherence to ethical standards.

This tale is based on documented facts and historical events that have transpired over the last 100 years. The story involves events that began during the First World War and have progressed to the present time. Some historical perspective will aid in the narration of the events that led to our cautionary tale. At the onset of the First World War, the German navy had developed and refined a new class of submersible warship, the submarine, commonly referred to as the U-boat. These naval war machines prowled the north seas around the British Isles, attacking the cargo ships and naval vessels of the Allies. At the beginning of the 20th century, England was the leading naval superpower. Coincidentally, during this time, the United States was undergoing a significant influx of immigrants from the British Isles and other parts of Europe. Since transatlantic travel was by way of ship, a profitable industry was created for travel between the two continents. The RMS *Lusitania* (Figure 0.1) was launched in 1906 and was a veteran of over 200 passages across the Atlantic Ocean. Hostilities between Germany and the Allies broke out and the First World War was declared on July 28, 1914. On August 4, 1914, the British declared war on Germany. On May 7, 1915, a German U-boat torpedoed the *Lusitania* on the starboard side just forward of the front boiler and beneath the wheelhouse of

FIGURE 0.1 *Lusitania.* (Library of Congress.)

the ship. Soon after the torpedo struck approximately 10 feet below the water line, a second explosion in the area of the torpedo strike caused the ship to sink within 18 minutes. The sinking occurred approximately 11 miles off the southern coast of Ireland which was a declared war zone.

The British claimed that the *Lusitania* was a non-military ship and that Cruiser Rules had been breached by the sinking, although the *Lusitania* had been equipped with a 6-inch concealed deck gun and was carrying hundreds of tons of war munitions. At the time of the sinking, the *Lusitania* was unarmed but was carrying munitions as verified in 1982 by the British Foreign Office. When the war broke out, the *Lusitania* was put on the armed merchant cruiser list by the British Admiralty.

Several conspiracy theories have been proposed throughout the years. Central to those theories is the question of how such a big ship equipped with watertight compartments sank so rapidly from a single torpedo strike and explosion. A main component of some of the conspiracy theories lies with the second explosion that was reported soon after the torpedo strike. This second explosion was reported to have occurred above the area of the torpedo strike and some attribute it to unlisted munitions in the cargo hold. The official cargo manifest lists 750 tons of various ammunitions, shrapnel artillery shells with buster chargers without propellant chargers or fuses. Patrick Beesly, a former British intelligence officer, has claimed that the cargo included 46 tons of aluminum powder, a component of explosives. Steven Danver claims that there was a large quantity of gun cotton (nitrocellulose). These items were not listed on the official cargo manifest. These unknown, alleged items, and presumptions, are ripe fodder for conspiracy theories and theorists.

One of the theorists, Gregg Bemis, who owns the wreck, has postulated a variety of scenarios that essentially deal with the secondary explosion which may be attributed to the detonation of a variety of explosive sources. These explosive sources are the detonation of aluminum powder, gun cotton detonation, coal dust explosion, or a boiler explosion. Mr Bemis favored the explosion produced by gun cotton. Among this list, aluminum powder and gun cotton would represent contraband munitions which fit the conspiracy theory of Gregg Bemis.

Lawrence Livermore Laboratories were contracted to perform experiments on the four possible scenarios. Their findings were as follows: Aluminum powder explosions produce a very bright detonation which is completely contrary to the eyewitness reports. This scenario was simply discredited because such an event was not witnessed. The gun cotton detonation experiment was contrary to the time delay observed between the first explosion produced by the torpedo and the second explosion as having occurred some 15–30 seconds later. The gun cotton explosion would immediately follow the first explosion. These two contraband munitions explosions simply did not fit the rest of the known data. Tests on a possible coal dust detonation did not produce sufficient power and would result in little structural damage. Again, a coal explosion was discounted as a possible contributory cause to the rapid sinking. The simulation of a boiler explosion fits the timeline between the two explosions and is in concert with eyewitness accounts, but a boiler explosion would not produce significant structural damage.

The Lawrence Livermore scientists concluded that it would also not be sufficient to increase the rate of sinking of the *Lusitania*. Their conclusion, based on mathematic simulations and computer-aided analysis, revealed that a six-foot breach of the hull caused by the torpedo would be sufficient to cause the sinking in approximately 18 minutes. Mr Bemis does not agree with the conclusions of the scientists at Lawrence Livermore.

From an ethical forensic engineering perspective, we can take some lessons from the sinking of the *Lusitania*. There is no documented evidence that contraband munitions were carried in the holds of the ship. Danver and Beesly offer no proof for the hypothesis of unlawful munitions. However, even if we assume that these munitions were on board, scientific tests disprove that such an event occurred because the second explosion did not immediately follow the torpedo explosion and it was not an extremely bright event.

The scenario that fits the witness statements, a boiler explosion, is summarily discounted by the conspiracy theorists because it is contrary to their non-scientific allegations. The scientific tests are also consistent with the sinking in the allotted time of 18 minutes, but are discounted by the conspiracists because they state that such computations are too complicated and there are too many unknowns. The allegation of too many unknowns and too complicated a problem is a typical allegation by forensic experts of all flavors who do not follow ethical standards. In most instances, these pseudo-forensic experts are incapable of carrying out sophisticated analysis, are too lazy, or are biased.

A linchpin of science and engineering is the scientific method. In summary, the scientific method is as follows. From observation, we develop a scenario of the events that have transpired. This scenario is the hypothesis. Based on this hypothesis, we perform calculations to describe the event. Further, we perform tests to validate the hypothesis and the calculations. If the tests and calculations are not in agreement with the hypothesis, we must modify the hypothesis to match the data. In the case of the *Lusitania*, the hypothesis that contraband munitions were responsible for the sinking of the ship was disproven. The scenario that matched the evidence was a boiler explosion. Furthermore, calculations on the inflow of sea water causing the sinking from the torpedo explosion were verified. To deny these results in a court of law as a forensic practitioner is unethical and does not meet engineering or scientific standards.

Preface

In the United States, the general population often associates and correlates *ethics* with *morals*. Morality and ethics are interwoven into the structure and fabric of our behavior. These concepts of virtuosity, it may be said, are held to be true in our general conduct and, in particular, in the scientific and legal system of our country. Ethics and morals have been interjected into the Judeo-Christian ethos which constitutes the generally accepted and proper conduct that overlays the scientific and legal community.

In recent years, a new term has surfaced that tends to give certain persons a higher standing in the scientific, legal, and political community with respect to the rest of the masses who encompass these fields. This term is described as the moral compass. This so-called moral compass is attributed to the good ones among us and is believed to guide our behavior in all facets of life. This moral authority term alludes to the propensity of good, just, pious persons to behave and do the proper deed. Just what that proper deed may be is a subject of debate in a particular field. Morality and ethics are actually two different and distinct concepts in the scientific and engineering forensic fields, which are the subjects of this book. Morality is not a concept that is covered in the book. Specifically, ethical behavior and concepts are the only concern in science and engineering.

It should be emphasized that ethics in forensic engineering and science have largely been unheeded, misused, misguided, misapplied, ignored, fudged, and generally ignored by a significant number of practitioners in these fields. Simply stated, the state of forensic science and engineering in the United States is in disarray, as described by the 2009 National Academy of Sciences (NAS) Report. The NAS Report, which was promulgated almost a decade ago, has attempted to make inroads into the corruption associated with these disciplines, but it is the authors' opinion that it has not made any significant progress because of the virulent opposition to standardization.

In this context, this book is intended to outline the state of the forensic sciences field with respect to recognized methods and the application of science, mathematics, and technology in the civil and criminal legal system in the United States. Significant emphasis is placed on the ethical role of the practicing forensic scientist when performing analysis, reports, and opinions associated with civil litigation and the criminal justice system. The effect of bias is also investigated as conceptualized by the forensic practitioner, the attorney, and the court. The role of these separate and distinct entities is analyzed and their effect scrutinized as they may lead to misconceptions and questionable science. Some common misconceptions and their relationship to actual cases are formulated and explained in the book.

The NAS Report covered a wide array of topics including biological evidence, analysis of controlled substances, friction ridge analysis (fingerprints), shoe prints and tire tracks, tool mark and firearms identification, analysis of hair evidence, analysis of fiber evidence, question document examination, analysis of paint and coating evidence, analysis of explosives evidence and fire debris, forensic odontology, bloodstain pattern analysis, and digital and multimedia analysis. The report did not cover forensic engineering analysis, the area with which the authors are most familiar. However, we do have some knowledge of areas that lend themselves to measurement and computation and can be described more rigorously with mathematics and physical laws. Thus, the book restricts the topics covered to those that may be quantized and mathematically analyzed.

In 2016, the President's Council of Advisors on Science and Technology (PCAST) submitted their report on Ensuring Scientific Validity of Feature-Comparison Methods to the president of the United States. The areas covered in the PCAST Report included DNA, bitemark analysis, latent fingerprint analysis, firearm analysis, footwear analysis, and hair analysis. The PCAST Report concluded that *there is a need for clarity about the scientific standards for the validity and reliability of forensic method, and the need to evaluate specific forensic methods to determine whether they have been scientifically established to be valid and reliable.* The PCAST Report was limited to "feature comparison" methods that attempt to determine the correlation between a sample and a known source.

REASONABLENESS

The National Institute of Justice (NIJ) has instituted a directive aimed at forensic scientists and attorneys working for federal governmental agencies who work in the varied federal laboratories to refrain from using the term *"to a reasonable degree of scientific certainty."* In our opinion, we applaud this directive. A better term suited to a scientist in the forensic or technical fields would be *"to a high degree of scientific or engineering certainty given the data available and considering the possible variability analysis that can be scientifically argued."* Let us explain the difference by taking a simple example.

A car skids out of control with the brakes locked on dry pavement. The question arises whether the vehicle was speeding in a 30 mile per hour zone, and both sides in the litigation are asked to investigate the question. The coefficient of friction for tires is well known on pavement. Let us say that its value is 0.7. Using this value, we could determine the speed of the vehicle based on the length of the skid marks. This leads to a speed of the vehicle of 50 miles per hour. In this example, the actual values are not important. The important factor is whether this value is to a high degree of certainty. An opposing expert opines that the value of the coefficient of friction is 0.3 and obtains a speed of the vehicle of say 25 miles per hour. The opposing expert argues that the number of skid marks, the baldness of the tires, and the condition of the suspension components led him to use the low frictional coefficient value. These conditions are, in his opinion, reasonable, when in fact they are unreasonable and unsupported by tests or inspections, and violate fundamental physical laws. Another more appropriate term is *junk science.* These conclusions by the opposing expert are not based on fundamental scientific or technical analysis, but rather on conjecture. Simply put, the data is made up to fit the client's need. The calculations may be correctly performed but the data used is completely incorrect. A careful investigator would have measured an appropriate coefficient of friction, inspected the tires and suspension system, and accurately measured all the physical evidence so that his conclusions would be to a *high degree of certainty.* A second method of analysis or possibly a third method may also be employed to corroborate the conclusions alluded to. This type of sleight of hand calculation is often seen and is highly unethical.

Audience

This book is intended to aid practicing forensic scientists and engineers in their formulation of a proper investigation leading to a report and conclusion which is scientifically valid and acceptable to the court system. The book describes the historical development of the court system and the rules of evidence. It describes methods and techniques in support of the challenge that may arise with respect to the application of the methods of science in litigation. The book covers most of the areas of forensic sciences with a few exceptions, including DNA, medicine, chemistry, biology, coroner issues, and investigations which cannot be quantified using mathematics and the scientific method. The areas covered include more of the physical sciences, which can be quantified through measurement and analysis with proper instrumentation.

The book places heavy emphasis on the use of standards, measurements, and calculations in the quest to reveal the truth in a forensic investigation. This type of process always leads to a systematic and ethical conclusion.

Acknowledgments

The authors wish to thank Mark Listewnik for his support and wisdom and for all the encouragement that he has provided throughout the preparation and development of this book. Additionally, the staff of Taylor & Francis provided valuable insight into the formulation of the topics and the arrangement of the chapters. Special thanks to Nanette Krueger for her insight and proofing of the manuscript.

Authors

Harold Franck founded Advanced Engineering Associates Inc. (AEA) in 1989 with a home office in Charleston, West Virginia and a satellite office in St. Petersburg, Florida. AEA is a forensic engineering investigative company that also performs a certain amount of design associated with losses. The main thrust of the company involves accident reconstruction, fire dynamic analysis, electrical incidents, structural distress, and biomechanics of injury. Harold holds a BSEE and MSEE from West Virginia University.

Darren Franck is president of AEA and has been with the company since 1995. Darren holds a BSCE from Virginia Polytechnic Institute and State University and an MSME from Georgia Institute of Technology and has extensive experience in 3D animations and simulations as applied to forensic cases. The principals of the company are registered professional engineers and have certificates of authority in Florida, Kentucky, Ohio, Michigan, North Carolina, Virginia, and West Virginia.

Symbols and Units

In this section, we list the common symbols used in science and engineering for quick reference. We have also listed common units used to perform scientific calculations. Note that, in many instances, units are in the English system (pound, foot, second) and other units are in the metric system (kilogram, meter, second), also known as SI. The section on conversion factors allows for easy conversion between the two systems. Unfortunately, in the United States, an attempt to convert all units to the metric system to follow the rest of the world did not succeed. Consequently, some conversions are necessary but relatively simple.

ϕ	Golden ratio of the Greeks = 1.618034...
xn	Fibonacci numbers = 0, 1, 1, 2, 3, 5, 8, 13,...
K_e	Kinetic energy (ft-lb)
w	Weight (lb or Kg)
g	Acceleration due to gravity (ft/s^2 or m/s^2)
v	Velocity (ft/s or m/s)
V	Volume (ft^3 or m^3 or gal or liters)
a	Acceleration (ft/s^2 or m/s^2)
d	Distance (ft or m)
F	Force (lb or Kg)
m	Mass (Kg or slugs or lb)
x, y, z	Distance in a particular direction (ft or m)
σ	stress
A	Area (ft^2 or m^2)
ε	Strain
d	Deformation
r	Density
l or L	Length (ft or m)
E	Young's modulus
t	Shearing stress
t	Thickness
P_n	Normal load
P_t	Transverse load
$\boldsymbol{v}$	Poisson's ratio
e	Dilation
p	Pressure
k	Bulk modulus
T	Torque
r	Radial distance

$\boldsymbol{J}$	Polar moment of inertia
G	Shear modulus
ϕ	Angle of twist
$\boldsymbol{I}$	Area moment of inertia
S	Section modulus
M	Moment
Q	First moment of inertia
V	Shear in the section
r	Radial arm
μ	Coefficient of friction
K	Effective length factor
SxP	Sensitivity of P to x
V_{xj}	Variability of x
x_{am}	Arithmetic mean
x_{gm}	Geometric mean
$\boldsymbol{a}_t$	Unit vector in the tangential direction
$\boldsymbol{a}_r$	Unit vector in the radial direction

Note vectors may be represented by an overscore notation or by a **bolded** symbol.

1

Introduction to Forensic Science

HISTORY

Forensic sciences were introduced into the mainstream public consciousness through the writings of Sir Arthur Conan Doyle in the latter part of the 19th century and the first part of the 20th century, through his main character Sherlock Holmes and his sidekick Dr Watson. Sherlock Holmes was the consummate detective and scientist. He relied on careful and detailed observation coupled with deduction to solve cases. Essentially, he utilized many of the components of the scientific method to find the culprit and absolve the innocent. Doyle was also an advocate of justice who personally investigated two cases leading to the exoneration of two men. Doyle was trained in medicine and credited one of his former teachers, Joseph Bell, as the inspiration for Sherlock Holmes. In contrast to his scientific training, Doyle was intrigued by spiritualism, freemasonry, and the paranormal. Although Doyle had the normal human biases and frailties, his main character, Holmes, did not. As a way of introduction to the book, we wish to look at the history of some of the forensic devices and techniques that have been and continue to be used. The items and techniques detailed are not all inclusive but have generated the most controversy from a scientific perspective. As the science of forensics continues to develop, serious problems have arisen putting some of the topics into the realm of conjecture, supposition, art, falsification, and pure hogwash. As with any discipline, charlatans, pseudoscientists, and snake oil salesmen have entered the field. What they propose and testify to in court proceedings is not science, as will be described in a later chapter.

Forensic science has also been denigrated by the media, television, and the cinematic industry.

These industries have been complicit in promulgating falsehoods for the sake of artful storytelling in the pursuit of profits. This is not to say that their purpose is to falsify forensic science, but to stretch the truth, blend pseudoscience into real science, and produce a product which exhilarates and thrills the audience. Although these are noble pursuits for entertainment purposes, they tend to cast a shadow on what is possible and what is not.

Forensic sciences are misunderstood by the general population. The common understanding by the person on the street is that forensics deals with death and DNA. While these topics are true to the belief, they are but a part of the varied topics in forensics. Webster's Dictionary defines forensic as derived from *forum* or marketplace. It is of, or suitable for, public debate, involving the application of scientific knowledge to legal matters. It is a debate or formal argument. It is the application of science to laws that are either criminal or civil. Note that the emphasis is on the application of scientific laws to determine the root cause or the conclusion that is derived from the analysis. It is not simply the argument for one side or another as was originally developed in Roman times. In those times, when a person was accused of a crime, the case was brought before public individuals in the forum where arguments for the guilt or innocence of the individual were determined by the best argument for either side.

Unfortunately, the consideration or determination of the best argument is sometimes utilized to arrive at a judgment, either civilly or criminally. The best argument may be firmly rooted in science or it may be on the fringes of science or simply not science at all. This is where ethical behavior enters the picture and where in the past, and continuing today, forensic sciences have been in flux and controversy. Sometimes, and for some specific examples of the various disciplines in forensics, the science and its methods simply do not adhere to testable, duplicatable, mathematically correct, and statistical determinable analysis. It is simply not ethical or scientifically correct to say that anything is possible. Possible outcomes must be rooted in science. It is always necessary to state the potential for error and the probability of the event.

As previously noted, the origins of forensic science are rooted in the criminal side. Criminal behavior has always been subject to prosecution in one form or another, whether the prosecution was just or not. Traditionally, the evidence was derived either from eyewitness descriptions or from confessions. Today, we know the pitfalls of coerced confessions and the inaccuracy of witness accounts of the events. Coerced confessions through *enhanced techniques* are sometimes referred to by advocates as necessary to obtain correct information. Needless to say, such techniques have been critically debunked on several levels. Similarly, many scientific studies on the accuracy of an eyewitness or a participant to an event show that they are simply not accurate. As a rule, in forensic scientific investigations, the authors consider the accounts of an eyewitness or involved party only as a last resort to see if their account fits the physical scientific evidence. Many so-called forensic experts rely too much on events or descriptions by observers in their analysis and conclusions. This is simply the wrong approach and is not consistent with the scientific method. On a lighter side, some common statements by involved parties include the following:

"It wasn't like that before."
"I just want what is owed to me."
"I was not speeding."
"The storm did all that damage."
"My back and neck hurt so much."
"I am innocent."
"I was not there."

Some of these statements may actually be true, but they are not in consort with science and should not be considered until they can be verified through careful data-based scrutiny.

A classical example of the false power of observation is demonstrated in the flat earth terra centric philosophy of earlier times. Animal life, and in fact all life on earth, is subject to circadian cycles. To refresh the reader's memory, recall that a circadian cycle deals with the response of life to the changes from day to night, hot and cold, tidal effects, and the change in the seasons. These cycles affect all life from microbes to plants and animals. For example, some plants and animals are nocturnal while others are not. It seems that most humans are not nocturnal.

So, as humanoids evolved, they noticed that the sun rises in the east, climbs through the sky, and sets in the west. That led to their observation and experience that as they lived on the land, they were stationary while the sun traversed the sky. The same observation followed for the night sky with the stars and the Milky Way taking a similar path. Their logical conclusion was that they were the center of their universe and the sun and stars revolved around them. This observation was true for all the celestial objects they witnessed, reinforcing their earth-centered hypothesis. However, some anomalies were noted with the retrogression of some of the planets as they traversed through the night sky. Since these aberrations in the planetary motion could not be explained, they were disregarded. Needless to say, their observations led them to the wrong conclusion because all the evidence was not included in their model of the cosmos. Although there was ample evidence from careful observations by early civilizations that the earth was not the center of the universe, it took a couple of millennia for the true nature to be revealed through the telescope and a heliocentric explanation that agreed with observation. Similarly, the flat earth hypothesis was not generally disproven until careful observation of shadows cast by the sun and, more significantly, confirmed by the telescopic observations of Galileo.

Eratosthenes was the first person to calculate the circumference of the earth more than 2000 years ago. This Greek astronomer, while living in Alexandria, Egypt, noted that the shadow of the sun in Alexandria never reached the bottom of the wells on a particular day of the year. However, in Syene, on the same day of the year, the sun reached the bottom of the wells indicating that it was directly above. By measuring the difference in the angle between the two cities, about 7°, Eratosthenes correctly concluded the curvature of the earth as a sphere. Consequently, relating the ratio of the angle of inclination (7° in 360°) to the distance between the two cities, approximately 500 miles, he obtained a value for the circumference of about 25,000 miles. We now know that the accepted value of the circumference of the earth is about 24,901 miles. His error was 0.397%, or roughly 4 parts in 1000. We would be lucky if some forensic practitioners were that good at analysis. Figure 1.1 is a view of the earth as seen from space.

We must be careful when we malign observation. Careful, critical observation is one very important component in science. Observations must be made in a controlled scientific manner. A detailed protocol is required when making meaningful observations. However, observations alone do not constitute science. Other components must be adhered to for an observation to hold up under critical scrutiny. We tend to emphasize the importance of

FIGURE 1.1 View of Earth. (Courtesy NASA.)

scientific observation because too many forensic investigators tend to rely too much on observation and witness statements. A reoccurring theme that is sometimes provided is "they claim that... and we need to consider the alleged claim as true in order to be thorough in our investigation."

At the beginning of the second millennium, circa 1200 AD, the Chinese began to use some science in the prosecution of justice. These cases involved medicine and entomology to solve cases. Indian and Chinese interrogators for the justice system examined mouths and tongues along with the amount of saliva to determine guilt or innocence. The thought was that guilty persons would have drier mouths than innocent persons. For what reason, no one knows.

In the 1700s, forensic sciences were further developed by the studies of violent deaths and their effect on humans. The involvement of weapons, footprints, and clothing marks, and the transfer of materials to crime scenes started to be studied. At this time, the beginnings of toxicology relative to poisonings and ballistics were also developed in Europe by German, French, and British investigators. In France, Alphonse Bertillon developed better techniques to identify individuals by the use of anthropometry to accurately describe the physical characteristics of individuals. This descriptive characterization of physical characteristics led to the development of fingerprint identification. Several researchers from India,

England, and the United States developed classification systems for fingerprints. By the early 1900s, fingerprints were commonly used for the identification of individuals. At this time, the Uhlenhuth test was also developed to differentiate human from animal blood with further refinements introduced in the 1960s by Maurice Muller. The crowning achievement in forensic sciences came about in the 1980s with the development of DNA. Since then, significant refinements and accuracy have been developed in the field of DNA. Today, DNA is essentially unquestioned as a scientific tool with an exceptional rate of success. Unfortunately, that is not the case for some forensic science disciplines.

In the areas of failure analysis, considerable advances have been made as a result of the increased use of technology, computers, and basic laws of physics. Today, we have a consistent understanding of the properties of materials, their propensity for failure, and their strength. Along with excellent mathematical models, most catastrophic occurrences can be accurately depicted and described. The areas of interest include the human body, vehicular collisions, and natural forces such as wind, rain, and snow and their effect on structures. Another area where advances have occurred is in fire dynamics and simulation. The investigation of fire development and corroboration by scientific tests provide deep insight into the evolution and destruction caused in a fire. The change of state in the materials in a fire is irreversible. Computer advances have enabled the development of simulation programs that can calculate dynamic processes with extreme accuracy and predictive capabilities. These techniques essentially make the analysis of fire development reversible from an analytical perspective. With these tools, investigators can now trace the fire development and more accurately determine the origin of a fire and the possible source of ignition. In the parlance of fire investigators, the origin and the cause (O&C) can be determined.

Similarly, tests conducted on structures and materials have produced a plethora of standards in the construction of vehicles, houses, and structures. Standards development continues as the science of failure analysis becomes more mature. Many organizations devoted to standards development continue to evolve and refine the documents they have created. It is heartening to see that cities and states across the United States have developed stricter enforcement and have driven the development of standards.

However, certain areas of forensic sciences are not science at all. More concisely, they may be pseudoscience, conjecture, experience, art, or something else. They have no basis in experimentation or mathematical calculations, and have not been subjected to peer review. However, these questionable areas in forensics are still allowed to be introduced and testified upon in courts of law in civil and criminal cases. In more instances than should be allowed, they have been responsible for incorrect criminal prosecutions that have led to long penal sentences and in some instances executions. We briefly touch upon some of the more egregious areas where there is a disconnect between actual science and forensic disciplines. In many of these areas, partial analysis, assumptions, misconceptions, erroneous or incorrect science, incorrect analysis, and untested hypothesis are the basis for the conclusions that are offered. In some instances, these conclusions are offered due to lack of knowledge or misunderstanding of science. In others, the conclusions are offered to bolster one side or the other of the forensic argument. To be clear, there are areas where scientific analysis varies to a certain extent because some of our scientific models are somewhat inaccurate. However, in many instances, the analysis and opinions offered are misleading, erroneous, and unethical.

Let us turn our attention to polygraph tests, commonly known as lie detector tests. The polygraph was invented circa 1921 by a medical student and police officer from Berkeley, California, by the name of John Larson. Through the years, several modifications and additions have been made to the original design. The theory behind a polygraph test centers on the physical response that a person undergoes when he or she answers questions that may be untruthful. Basically, as the theory or hypothesis implies, the response to deceptive answers will differ from the response to truthful answers in terms of the physiological characteristics produced by the respondent. Common physiological responses measured are pulse rate, blood pressure, respiration rate, and skin conductivity or perspiration. Polygraph tests have a certain amount of reliability and are often used as a tool to determine if the individual being investigated is being truthful. Although the figures vary, the accuracy of lie detector tests is in the 75% accuracy range. It is well known that individuals are capable of misleading the equipment and the interrogator so that the polygraph is not allowed as evidence in court.

The concept behind the polygraph is that when questioned, the individual will react physiologically, that is, measured pulse rate, perspiration, etc., will change when the subject is lying rather than telling the truth. However, research on the reactions to polygraph examinations shows no specific physiological markers with the truth or with a lie. Essentially, the brain activity and its related markers are unknown and not measurable at this point in time. Some claim that the accuracy of the polygraph examination is as high as 90%, which has not been proven and the National Research

Council has not validated this effectiveness. In fact, in their findings, the Supreme Court summarized that the usefulness of the polygraph was akin to flipping a coin. In a further fact, the use of the polygraph, as with other questionable forensic sciences (i.e. fingerprints, tool marks, tire impressions, etc.), is subjective and prone to the interpretation of the examiner. As such, bias may be introduced, relegating polygraph examinations to the pseudosciences. In 2003, the National Academy of Sciences concluded that the majority of polygraph research was *"unreliable, unscientific, and biased."* One must wonder why the courts do not allow polygraph evidence as inaccurate as it is, yet allow similarly unreliable evidence such as tool marks, partial fingerprints, and other so-called forensic scientific disciplines in court testimony.

2

The State of Forensic Sciences

INTRODUCTION

How did forensic sciences reach such a state of disarray? There are no clear or conclusive reasons for this predicament. Part of the answer may lie in the dichotomy between the civil and the criminal elements presented in the courts. Civil courts do not mandate restrictive penal sentences, although they may mandate monetary resolution for a case. In contrast, in a criminal case, the judgment may involve either incarceration or parole and, in some cases, monetary restitution to the aggrieved parties. In the direst of cases, the death sentence may be imposed. Often, the trial rules in criminal and civil cases vary. For example, a firearms expert may be asked to testify in a civil matter whether a revolver was properly designed and/or somehow malfunctioned and caused injury. Alternatively, that same expert may testify in a criminal case whether that particular revolver was used in a murder investigation. In the most general sense, forensic experts may testify in civil and/or criminal cases.

The question that immediately arises is whether the rules of evidence for both cases are the same. The science that was used to determine the civil case, whether the gun was properly designed, involves forces, machine design, tooling practices, strength of materials, and ballistic performance, to name a few. In the criminal elements of a case, the firearms expert is asked whether that particular gun fired the lethal or injurious bullet. These are two separate and distinct issues for many reasons.

The most obvious reason is that in the design of a weapon or a tool, well-established physical laws are employed. These laws are constantly utilized and agree in repeatable tests; are published in a plethora of texts, scientific articles, and scientific organizations; and are recognized by the entire scientific community. For example, variability in data is well established such as the variation in the hardness properties of 304 stainless steel versus 316 stainless steel. In actuality, the differences in the two steels can be gleaned from tables and graphs and, if the investigator wishes, may also be verified through his own hardness tests on the two materials. To state that a particular revolver fired the particular projectile is by no means a clear-cut conclusion and is not based on science, as will be expounded in a later chapter of the book. For the time being, we simply state that there are insufficient scientific tests and data to support the conclusion that is offered whether a particular weapon was used to perpetrate a crime. The theory with which such a conclusion can be made is that tooling marks are unique. A particular tool making a mark on a surface at a particular time is distinct from the tool making a mark on a similar surface at another time. Additionally, it is claimed that two identically designed and constructed tools make distinct and individual tool marks on a particular surface. For example, it is claimed that two identical revolvers striking the hammer against a cartridge will produce unique and different imprint marks on the rear surface of the cartridge. A preposterous conclusion! To our knowledge, no such uniqueness has been tested, proven, or validated in double-blind studies by independent investigators. All that is needed to show that this uniqueness property does not exist is to show one example where the alleged theory fails. If that event occurs, the uniqueness theory fails and must be disregarded or modified. Consider the following scenario.

Legend has it that Isaac Newton developed his universal theory of gravitational attraction while observing apples falling from trees. Nice story with a ring of truth. What if some of the observations did not support this phenomenon? Let us say that on average one in a hundred times the apples flew upward away from the earth. Would

Newton's theory be correct? It might be in most cases but not in all. This is exactly what occurred when scientists attempted to predict the location of Mercury as it revolved around the sun. Newton's laws did not correctly predict the location because according to Einstein, massive bodies such as the sun actually distort space-time so that it is necessary to utilize Einstein's General Theory of Relativity to compute the orbit of Mercury. Newton's laws fail because of the curvature of space-time. Effectively, the massive sun compared to Mercury, a much smaller body, distorts space-time and affects the orbit. The closer the small object relative to the large object, the more influence that is observed in the orbit of the small object.

In essence, obtuse special cases need to be explained by science. Science is an explanation of what we observe. Science allows us to describe, with caveats, the phenomenon before us. However, it does not allow us to make extraordinary generalizations without extraordinary proof backed by extraordinary well-tested theories. Extraordinary claims require extraordinary proof as stated by Carl Sagan.

Another reason for the distinction in the issues involves the difference in the standard applied in civil versus criminal cases. Sometimes, a lax interpretation of the rules is allowed in civil cases but not in criminal cases or vice versa. Other times, experience supplants science and is allowed as scientific testimony. The rules for testimony in a Circuit or District Court may differ from a State or Federal Court. The opinion or ruling of a particular judge may differ from another justice of the court. One expert may be well known to a particular judge and be given preferential treatment and laxity in his testimony. After all, we are human and subject to our prejudices and preferences. It is very difficult to remove the human element from the judgmental equation. It is much easier to remove the human element from the mathematical or scientific truth. As a consequence, when an expert offers their opinion based on experience alone, it should not carry any more weight than the opinion of a lay person. A practitioner in the forensic sciences must conform to the rules mandated by scientific protocols based on the scientific method. Otherwise, to offer an opinion not based on science is simply lay testimony and should not be considered. It is unethical of the practitioner to do so. Therein lies the dichotomy in the separation and distinction of the issues.

SOME HISTORICAL PERSPECTIVE

Our basic system of justice is predicated upon the English system of justice which dates back to the Magna Carta in 1215. The Magna

Carta was influenced by King Henry I who specified that a limitation would be placed on certain of his powers. This limit resulted from, and was influenced by, the Charter of Liberties of 1100. After 1215, the Magna Carta underwent many modifications, and by the time the early settlers reached New England, it was influential in their interpretation of law. As a direct consequence, the Magna Carta played an influential role in the development of the Constitution of the United States. The Englishmen who colonized America were greatly influenced by the Magna Carta when they established their charters. These included the Virginia Charter, the Maryland Charter, and the Massachusetts Bay Company Charter. These early colonists' interpretation of the Magna Carta was anachronistic in that they believed that it guaranteed trial by jury and habeas corpus and was a fundamental law. Habeas corpus essentially means "you have the body" and relates to the direction to the prison warden to produce the person so that the court can determine the status and legality of the custody of the prisoner. The court order concerning the production of the habeas corpus is known as a writ.

Consequently, the framers of the constitution designed the legal system in the manner of English common law and the philosophy of John Locke who is regarded as the *Father of Classical Liberalism*. The significant influence of John Locke on the development of the founding documents of the United States cannot be underestimated. Locke was a true believer in empirical data in consort with the underpinnings of the beliefs of Francis Bacon. John Locke was extremely influential in social contract theory, liberal theory, and republicanism, and their significance on the Declaration of Independence, the Bill of Rights, and the United States Constitution. Locke's ideas on liberty, social contract, property, price theory, monetary thought, political theory, religious beliefs, and the concept of self, influenced many of the founding fathers of this country.

Francis Bacon was a man of many talents and best known through his seminal work *Novum Organum*. Through this work, Bacon emphasized a particular approach to scientific examinations based on careful observation and induction. Thus, he is regarded as the father of the *scientific method*. With regard to law, Bacon had considerable influence on the drafting of the *Napoleonic Code* and many reforms that were introduced into law by Prime Minister Robert Peel. These reforms essentially encased the relevance of the principles of evidence and logic in court proceedings.

Among many of his contributions, John Locke is known for his concept of empiricism, which states that knowledge is determined only by the experience of the person from which he or she perceives. His ideology relates to the science in observations that are capable of being tested and repeated. Further, he believed that nothing would be exempt from being disproven. These concepts are very important and critical when they relate to all science and in particular to our topic of forensic sciences.

It is important to make a distinction at this point. Although we have alluded to the contributions of John Locke with regard to the term empiricism, we need to clarify the point. Empiricism is derived from the term empirical which is defined as based on experiment or experience. Here is where the distinction needs to be made. If a forensic practitioner bases an opinion solely on his experience, that opinion cannot be considered as science. If the opinion is based on a plethora of robust experiments and the scientific literature along with his tests and experiments, then this is science and not just an opinion. Consider the following. I, as a researcher, wish to determine if horses are capable of being ridden. I perform a multitude of tests based on my attempts to ride many horses and every time an attempt is made, I get thrown. I then get called to a tribunal to offer my opinion on whether horses can be ridden, in which I state, *"In my opinion and experience, horses are not capable of being ridden."* Does this sound ridiculous? Of course it does, but it is no different from some of the junk science that is being proposed by some forensic investigators. The reasons for this preposterous conclusion are obvious. Other researchers don't agree with my conclusion. They know that with some fundamental training of the horse and rider, horses are quite easy to ride. Maybe I should have researched the subject further to determine if horses could be ridden. The only conclusion I could offer is, *"I can't ride a horse."*

Areas in forensic science that have not been properly tested, do not adhere to scientific principles, and violate the scientific method, cannot be methodically quantified, and are readily subject to bogus and unethical perversions. Unfortunately, many of these perversions have been introduced into the civil and criminal court system in the United States.

THE COURT SYSTEM

There are three main levels of court system in the United States. At the top level is the Supreme Court of the United States. Under this level are the sublevels of the Federal Court system referred to as Federal District Courts. At the next level are the individual State Supreme Courts. These State Courts are also made up of lower levels and include the District and County Courts of the states. Litigation generally begins at the lowest level, the County Courts. The litigation then proceeds to the State District Courts and to the

State Supreme Courts. Thereafter, the litigation may work its way up through the Federal Court system and eventually end up in the Supreme Court of the United States.

The Supreme Court is made up of eight justices appointed by the president and confirmed by the Senate. The chief justice is the ninth member, who is appointed and confirmed in the same manner as the other justices. The other justices are referred to as associate justices. Their appointment is for life and consequently may sway the opinions of the court in significant directions toward liberalism or conservatism. The cases heard by the Supreme Court are limited each year by the justices and proceed from Federal or State Courts. In other words, appeals may arise from Federal District Courts or from State Supreme Courts. There are 13 Federal District Circuit Courts of Appeal. These Federal Appeal Courts arise from 94 federal judicial districts of which 12 are regional Circuit Courts. The thirteenth federal district has jurisdiction over specialized cases relative to International Trade and the Court of Federal Claims. There are 50 State Supreme Courts. Figure 2.1 shows the US Courts of Appeal and District Courts.

Individual cases which may involve a practicing forensic biomechanical engineer would most probably not involve the opinions of the expert unless the case involves constitutional issues as with the Daubert case. The Supreme Court is the final arbiter of federal constitutional law and was established by the Constitution in 1789 in Article Three. These cases involve attorneys who present oral arguments on the merits of the case, and the forensic expert does not testify but his opinions may be cited.

The 50 State Supreme Courts are, in their function, essentially identical to the Federal Supreme Court system in that they normally hear appeals and do not make any finding of facts. When the State Supreme Courts find errors in a particular state decision, they will order the court to retry the case. The case is remanded to the lower court. The State Supreme Courts vary in their makeup depending on the particular constitution of the state in which they reside. These courts are distinct from Federal Courts in the same or similar geographic boundary. In some instances, appeals from these courts may end up in the United States Supreme Court if there is a question of law under the Constitution of the United States. The composition of the State Supreme Courts varies widely from the number of justices, their term length, and the method by which they are selected. Term lengths for these justices vary widely from 6 years to life terms. The number of justices also varies from five to nine. The modes by which the justices are selected include appointment by the governor, elected by the legislature, partisan or non-partisan election, and the Missouri Plan. The Missouri Plan originated

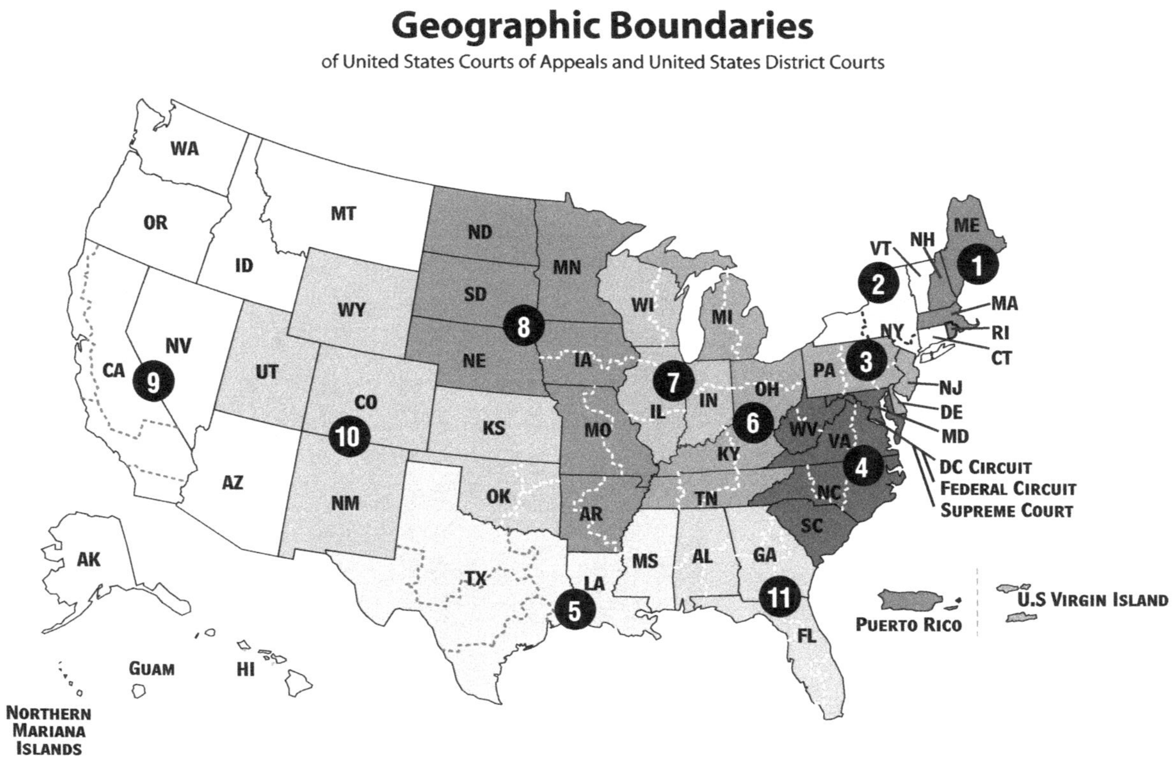

FIGURE 2.1 Geographic boundaries of United States Courts of Appeal and United States District Courts.

in 1940 in which a non-partisan commission reviews candidates and sends a list to the governor who has 60 days to decide. If the governor does not make the decision, the commission makes the selection. After 1-year service, the justice must stand in a retention election. If the judge fails to win a majority vote, the judge is removed from office and the process is repeated. Again, the expert does not testify in these courts, but his opinion may be cited by the attorneys presenting their legal arguments.

The composition of the State Courts varies widely. These courts are divided into three courts, beginning at the general jurisdiction level, sometimes called the Court of First Instance. According to each state, they may be made up of districts, counties, circuits, superior, municipal, or supreme designations. After the First Instance Courts, there are usually intermediate courts, referred to as Courts of Appeals or Appellate Courts. Some states do not have this intermediate level of Appellate Courts, but most do. The final court at the state level is the Supreme Court.

Consequently, the role of the expert resides in his or her testimony at the district level. This testimony is given in County Courts, Municipal Courts, and Circuit Courts at the lowest level of the judicial system in the State and the Federal Courts. Because of the diverse nature of jurisdictions, the acceptability of the testimony of the expert also varies widely. Many courts allow an expert to simply have knowledge which is greater than that of a lay person. Other courts, especially at the federal level, expect the expert to have significant knowledge and expertise far beyond the knowledge of a lay person. This scrutiny of the expert's credentials and testimony also varies widely depending on the nature of the case.

RULES OF EVIDENCE

Rules of evidence vary from state to state. In essence, most states have the same rules with some minor modifications. Generally, all rules of evidence are consistent with the Federal Rules of Evidence. However, this consistency is not always true. Traditional rules of evidence are composed of four types: real, demonstrative, documentary, and testimonial. From a general perspective, these four types of evidence must conform to the general rules of admissibility. The basic prerequisite for the admissibility of the four types of evidence is whether they are relevant, material, and competent.

- To be relevant, the item of evidence needs to have a tendency to increase the likelihood of the fact for which it is offered. Relevant evidence has the tendency to make a fact to prove or

disprove the probability of the allegation. Whether the evidence is strong or weak is to be decided by the finder of fact. Even if the relevant evidence is weak, it may be admitted unless it is deemed incompetent or is in conflict with an exclusionary rule.
- To be material, the evidence is offered to prove a fact which may be an issue in the case. The concept of whether the evidence is material is generally included in the concept of its relevance to the case.
- To be competent, the evidence that is being offered must meet traditional requirements of reliability. Generally, competent evidence along with relevant and material evidence for admissibility is referred to as foundational evidence. For the forensic expert, competent evidence may be used to show prior bad acts in a case to impeach the credibility of the forensic witness. If the forensic expert performed an unethical act in a previous case, the court may rule that the probative value of the evidence offered by the expert is prejudicial and may cause improper harm.

Let us now turn our attention to the different types of evidence and their distinctions and similarities and how their admissibility applies. To be admissible, all evidence must be relevant, material, and competent. In order to establish these prerequisites, a foundation is called for and the materiality, relevance, and competence must show what it actually is. In simple terms, the evidence must be authenticated. For *real evidence*, this can be accomplished in the following manners.

- Usually a witness is used to identify a particular object in court.
- Additionally, a witness may authenticate the object by distinctive markings such as a signature. This method avoids any discrepancies in the chain of custody of the object that may arise.
- The third method of authentication of the object is to provide the chain of custody, which must address the location of the object at all times. If the chain is broken, the evidence will generally be excluded. It must also be established that the evidence has not been altered in any manner.

For *demonstrative evidence*, the descriptive term summarizes what it is. It shows, demonstrates, or illustrates the testimony of the particular witness. Some examples are

- Maps, diagrams, animations
- Calculations, graphs, charts
- Photographs, videos, recordings

Real evidence may be in the form of *documentary evidence*. When documents are used, they must be authenticated in the same manner as real evidence with a proper chain of custody. Care must be taken with documentary evidence because this type of evidence may contain hearsay. Hearsay is generally excluded. Many documents are self-authenticating, such as certified copies of public records, newspapers, or certificates of business records. In certain cases, summaries or compilations of voluminous records may be allowed where the originals are authenticated by the opposing parties.

The last form of evidence is *testimonial evidence*. Testimony is the most basic form of evidence and does not necessarily require another form of evidence as a prerequisite for its admissibility. Normally, the court decides if the witness is competent based on the following criteria:

- The witness must take an oath or attest to the truth.
- The witness must have personal knowledge not hearsay.
- The witness must remember what was perceived of the event.
- The witness must be able to adequately communicate what was perceived.

This is a brief summary of the generally accepted rules of evidence used in the United States from the perspective of the forensic sciences expert. There are many other rules that generally apply to the attorneys and the courts, but those are not the purview of the forensic expert. For clarity, the Federal Rules are outlined below. Rule 701 relates to the Opinion Testimony by Lay Witnesses. The testimony by expert witnesses is summarized in Rule 702 of the Federal Rules of Evidence and states the following:

Rule 702—Testimony by Expert Witnesses

A witness who is qualified as an expert by knowledge, skill, experience, training, or education may testify in the form of an opinion or otherwise if

(a) the expert's scientific, technical, or other specialized knowledge will help the trier of fact to understand the evidence or to determine a fact issue;
(b) the testimony is based on sufficient facts or data;
(c) the testimony is the product of reliable principles and methods; and
(d) the expert has reliably applied the principles and methods to the facts of the case.

Some other rules that may apply are listed below. These include portions of Rules 703 through 706.

Rule 703—Bases of an Expert

An expert may base an opinion on facts or data in the case that the expert has been made aware of or personally observed. If experts in the particular field would reasonably rely on those kinds of facts or data in forming an opinion on the subject, they need not be admissible for the opinion to be admitted. But if the facts or data would otherwise be inadmissible, the proponent of the opinion may disclose them to the jury only if their probative value in helping the jury evaluate the opinion substantially outweighs their prejudicial effect.

Rule 704—Opinion on an Ultimate Issue

(a) **In General—Not Automatically Objectionable**. An opinion is not objectionable just because it embraces an ultimate issue.
(b) **Exception**. In a criminal case, an expert witness must not state an opinion about whether the defendant did or did not have a mental state or condition that constitutes an element of the crime charged or of a defense. Those matters are for the trier of fact alone.

Rule 705—Disclosing the Facts or Data Underlying an Expert

Unless the court orders otherwise, an expert may state an opinion—and give the reason for it—without first testifying to the underlying facts or data. But the expert may be required to disclose those facts or data on cross-examination.

Rule 706—Court-Appointed Expert Witnesses

(a) **Appointment Process**. On a party's motion or on its own, the court may order the parties to show cause why the expert witness should not be appointed and may ask the parties to submit nominations. The court may appoint any expert that the parties agree on and any of its own choosing. But the court may only appoint someone who consents to act.
(b) **Expert's Role**. The court must inform the expert of the expert's duties. The court may do so in writing and have a copy filed with the clerk or may do so orally at a conference in which the parties have the opportunity to participate. The expert:

(1) must advise the parties of any findings the expert makes;
(2) may be deposed by any party;
(3) may be called to testify by the court or any party;
(4) may be cross-examined by any party, including the party that called the expert.

(c) **Compensation**. The expert is entitled to a reasonable compensation, as set by the court. The compensation is payable as follows:
(1) in a criminal case or in a civil case involving just compensation under the Fifth Amendment, from any funds that are provided by law; and
(2) in any other civil case, the parties in the proportion and at the time that the court directs—and the compensation is then charged like other costs.

(d) **Disclosing the Appointment to the Jury**. The court may authorize disclosure to the jury that the court appointed the expert.

(e) **Parties' Choice of Their Own Experts**. This rule does not limit a party in calling its own experts.

THE NATIONAL ACADEMY OF SCIENCES (NAS) REPORT

"Strengthening Forensic Science in the United States: A Path Forward" is the title of the 2009 report by the National Research Council's Committee on Identifying the Needs of the Forensic Sciences Community. This report is commonly referred to as the NAS Report and incorporates input from the National Academy of Sciences, the National Academy of Engineering, the Institute of Medicine, and the National Research Council. According to the report, significant improvements are needed in the forensic sciences. Many of the improvements in the report deal with the lack of resources, policies, funding, the court system, standardization, statistics, law, litigation both civil and criminal, training, laboratory practices, scientific disciplines, and ethical standards.

Some of the areas covered in the NAS Report are not ethical issues covered in this book because the authors have no knowledge of those subjects. These include DNA, serology, chemicals, coatings, hair, fibers, infrastructure, training and education, coroner and medical examiner systems, budgeting, accreditation, licensing, and certification. The areas that are addressed in this book include measurable evidence with respect to physics, tooling, corrosion/rapid oxidation, forces, impressions, and rates of error which are best characterized as uncertainty and sensitivity. Some of the areas in forensic science are laboratory based, others are based on expert interpretation of observed patterns, while others are based on sound repeatable physical methods and computations. Our discussions center on the so-called expert interpretation and physical methods and related computations that form those expert interpretations. The interpretation of the evidence usually involves matching a particular characteristic of the evidence to some known sample. For example, the match may be to a fingerprint based on a partial fingerprint found at a crime site. The match is then reported based on a few points comparing the partial to the full fingerprint. Among the 13 recommendations in the NAS Report, this book deals with Recommendation 9:

The National Institute of Forensic Science (NIFS), in consultation with its advisory board, should establish a national code of ethics for all forensic science disciplines and encourage individual societies to incorporate this national code as part of their professional code of ethics. Additionally, NIFS should explore mechanisms of enforcement for those forensic scientists who commit serious ethical violations. Such a code could be enforced through a certification process for forensic scientists.

In the areas of engineering and science, the development of codes of ethics represents the recognized behavior of those individuals who practice in the field. These codes guide the individual practitioner in the development of their theories on a particular case based on the proven, tested, repeated, confluence of the scientific knowledge, mathematical correctness, and formulation of their results. Let us see how this may apply to a variety of topics including tool marks, firearm marks, fingerprints, and even birth dates. These topics may be considered with respect to bias that presents itself when humans are asked or wish to make a determination based on their experience.

Cognitive science is the study of cognition. Cognition is the process of knowing or perceiving, or an idea. As such, our ideas or perceptions can easily lead us to faulty or incorrect conclusions which may be unethical at worst, or misinterpreted at best. Either way, they are incorrect and should never be offered in a forensic context. Unfortunately, many of these conclusions are routinely offered as fact under the label of science.

Let us look briefly at a topic covered in the NAS Report. The report discusses the issue of cognitive bias in which humans will tend to see patterns that may not actually exist. They present the case where students in statistical classes are asked in an introductory course the following question: How many people must be in a room in order for two of them to have the same birth date with a 50% probability? The birth date is considered as the day and the month of the year. The year is not considered and leap years are excluded along with any variations in the weekdays or the seasons. Actually, these variations in the seasons and weekdays are of little consequence in the analysis.

Intuitively, you might say that since there are 365 days in a year, you might need about half that number or about 180 people. Surely, 100 people is a pretty large number. The actual number is 23. The actual probability, P(A), is computed from the probability that no two people have the same birth date, P(A′). For example, for 23 people, the probability that no 2 people have the same birth date is

$$P(A') = \frac{365}{365} \times \frac{364}{365} \times \frac{363}{365} \times \ldots \times \frac{343}{365} \approx 0.4927$$

or

$$P(A) = 1 - P(A') \approx 0.5073$$

Of 23 people in a room, there is a 50% chance that 2 of them will have the same birth date. The following table shows the probability for some numbers of people and defies our intuition.

Number of People	Probability (%)
1	0.0
5	2.7
10	11.7
20	41.1
23	50.7
30	70.6
40	89.1
50	97.0
70	99.9

Consider the case of a fingerprint analyst who is attempting to make a determination on a partial print. He or she finds 10 points that match a sample print from a suspect. Maybe they also find another 10 features that do not match. What is the conclusion? What about the other portions of the fingerprint that they cannot analyze because those portions are not apparent on the partial print? Can a determination on the validity of the match be made with any certainty? The same argument can be applied to the striations on a bullet. These are called lands and grooves and are produced by the rifling in the barrel of the weapon. Rifling in the barrel is introduced to create spin on the bullet. Spin, or rotation, along the longitudinal axis creates a straighter path for the bullet, increasing the accuracy of the shot. These features are alleged to be unique. That is, two bullets fired from the same gun will be identical and bullets fired from different guns will always be different. Furthermore, only a portion of the striations are normally analyzed to see if they match a test bullet from the same weapon. What percentage of the striations are analyzed? Is it 10% or 50%? Can you state with any degree of certainty that analyzing 50% of some feature uniquely identifies a weapon or a person? In science, you cannot. Flip a coin. Heads you are free, tails you are guilty. Not very convincing odds. What if 9 out of 10 striations match and 1 does not? Can you say with certainty that the bullet came from a particular weapon? At best, you might be able to say that the probability was about 90% that it came from the particular weapon. Is it ethical, in such a case, to exclude all other weapons?

CONCLUSIONS

The examples cited in this chapter are but a few of those that distinguish the disarray in the state of forensic science in the United States. Hopefully, this chapter will aid in the illumination of the state of forensic science at this date. It is clear that a large portion of forensic science is not science at all. It is opinion, conjecture, limited experience, forgery, pseudoscience, snake oil salesmanship, fraud, gamesmanship, win at all costs, disregard for evidence that does not fit a particular position, and simply unethical. Ethics in science requires that all evidence must be included to support a particular scientific opinion. Data that does not fit must be examined and corollaries developed. All exceptions must be recorded and quantified, and parameters set to accommodate the exceptions.

3

The Role of Science

FORENSIC SCIENCE

While it is true that theory and science are closely related, it is necessary to make a clear distinction in some cases. Let us begin by properly defining a term in science known as a *law*. As an example, consider some well-known laws, referred to as Newton's laws. Three laws are attributed to Newton. These three laws allowed Newton to formulate the Theory of Gravitational Attraction we have all been exposed to. In general, we refer to this field of study as Newtonian Mechanics. Recall the undocumented story of the apple falling from the tree that Newton supposedly observed, which led him to his monumental discovery. In actuality, there is no direct or indirect evidence that a falling apple actually aided Newton in formulating his three laws. The falling apple is simply a myth, like many of the forensic sciences disciplines. Gravitational attraction allows us to compute with extreme accuracy the behavior and interaction of bodies at the macroscale. In most instances, we can use Newtonian mechanics to predict the paths and positions of the planets with great precision. We can launch rocket ships, and fire bullets and cannon balls and predict where they will strike the target with superlative accuracy. This is true except in the case of massive bodies affecting the orbit of a close small object, as explained in Chapter 2 with respect to Mercury. Similarly, in the largest scales of the universe, the laws formulated by Newton don't seem to yield the observational results.

Moreover, for some objects such as electrons, Newton's laws do not apply. We cannot use these laws to predict the location of electrons with any degree of accuracy. There are other fundamental principles that apply for subatomic particles at the microscale. There are separate and distinct laws that govern the field of Quantum Mechanics and General Relativity. In this field of study, we can only infer probabilities with respect to position and momentum relative to the observer of these subatomic particles. Similarly, general relativity, as postulated by Albert Einstein, explains phenomenon such as gravitational lensing created by the effect of very massive objects. There is also a nascently emerging field of gravity and its interactions at the extreme scale of the cosmos. This field is called Dark Energy and Dark Matter. This field of study is in its infancy and is derived from some observations which do not fit known phenomena at the cosmic level. These observations that disagree with the present conventional theories of the cosmos beautifully exemplify science and the evolution of knowledge. Essentially, a robust and concise theory or law places restrictions on its limits. The theory or law may be applied within the parameters dictated by the law or theory.

Let us backtrack and look at the state of physics over the past 300 years and see how science has evolved. We need not go back any further in time because at the time of Newton we already knew that the earth was not the center of the universe. Science at that time dictated that the known planets and the earth revolved around the sun. For about 200 years, Newton's laws gave a surprisingly accurate description of our limited knowledge of the universe. As further analysis and observation developed, it was necessary to incorporate the ideas of Einstein to describe the universe. One surprising observation by Edwin Hubble, that the universe was expanding and was much larger than previously known, emerged in the 1920s. Further developments ensued to describe and explain the very small and the very large components of the observable universe by Pauli, Schrodinger, Plank, Rutherford, Bohr, Heisenberg, Dirac, Oppenheimer, Feynman, and many others. Recent developments through observation of the deep cosmos indicate the presence of dark matter and dark energy which may explain the expansion of the universe and the rotational characteristics of galaxies along with the large-scale clustering of matter that is observed. Currently, these observations cannot be explained and, as stated previously, restrict our scientific knowledge.

It may be necessary to have three separate theories and corresponding laws to describe the universe at the very small scales, at the intermediate scales that we as humans experience, and at the very large scales of the universe. However, heroic attempts have been undertaken over the past 50 years to unify physical laws from the very small to the very large. This is the unsolved problem of finding a quantum theory that is consistent with general relativity or a quantum gravity theory. At the present time we can accurately describe these physical processes within the limitations we impose. Let us be clear, physical laws work extremely well at our observational level—that is what we as humans experience. We only ask forensic science to adhere to this level of understanding science and apply it to its particular discipline.

We don't require forensic science to conform to the subatomic or cosmological levels. We just need forensic science to adhere to the basic tenets of science, observation, experiment, theory, and confirmation. Confirmation arises from experimentation and documentation through rigorous studies.

The distinction between a law and a *theory* is as follows. Theories are generally derived from known laws. They essentially use known laws to make certain predictions. As the definition clearly states, a theory may be a speculation formulated from some underlying principle of an observed phenomena, a known law. Clearly, at this point in our discussion, with the appropriate caveats, we can state that Newtonian mechanics, general relativity, and quantum theory are well established and can be classified as *laws*. Dark matter and energy are fledgling theories at best and cannot be considered to describe the phenomenon that is being observed. There are simply too many unknowns and competing theories to define the events we observe at the grand scale of the cosmos.

Consequently, mature theories, such as quantum theory, can essentially be considered as laws unless they are disproven at a future date. Since quantum theory has withstood the test of time for almost 100 years, it seems reasonable that it is essentially a scientific law. How does this discussion relate to forensic science we wonder?

First and foremost, the name explains the dilemma that is present in the ethical considerations before the forensic science community. In order to adhere to scientific dogma and scrutiny, a theoretical postulation by a forensic scientist must conform to the strict definition of a law or theory. In order to do so, a method has been established by the scientific community over the past 300 years that is referred to as the Scientific Method. This topic will be extensively covered in Chapter 4.

At this juncture, we need to differentiate between science, experience, opinion, and art. We begin by considering the term art as an anathema. Why is art in the forensic sciences an anathema? Because an anathema is a thing greatly detested and art is human creativity or a specific skill or its application. Art is simply not science. Some protagonists have tried to introduce terms such as the art and science of engineering, for example, into the forensic sciences. While it is true that art and beauty may be portions of an engineering design, a description of an event, or a representation of some facts, art and beauty are without any concrete, observable, reproducible, data or analysis. Art and beauty are restricted to the observer. Some people consider most of the work by Picasso to be beautiful, others don't. Others think the works of Michelangelo to be artful, others may not. Science is cold hard facts, indisputable within the limitations imposed.

THEORIES

How do theories arise? This is a hard question to answer. We are not talking here about alien visitations to earth by extra-terrestrials, or abominable snowmen. We are talking about some alleged physical phenomenon that is postulated by an "expert" observer. Take a simple example such as a tool mark. The claim is that tools make unique marks. We can all agree that if we cut a log with a saw rather than with an axe, the nature of the cut is different and not arguable. The claim is that the marks produced by two identical knives will produce distinct marks that can be identified by trained observers. This claim is generally said to be true when a trained examiner analyzes the tool marks with a microscope. A similar claim is made with respect to lands and grooves made on the bullet fired by a particular gun, or the cartridge that is ejected from that gun. Additionally, the firing pin imprint on the casing is claimed to be unique. What about an identical gun? Could an identical gun from the same production run and for the same usage have made the tool marks? So, it seems reasonable to ask the question, where are the double-blind scientific tests and experiments? Is this theory true for caliber 9 mm Glocks produced between certain dates from factory X and not true for these guns produced on other dates?

Another theory is that fingerprints or at least partial fingerprints are unique. What about partial fingerprints from related individuals? Let us explain. Those of us who are parents realize, through observation, that our children inherit certain features from each parent. For example, the son has dad's feet or toes, or his thumbs are almost identical. What about partial features of their fingerprints? Are there any similarities or identicalities between these partial prints within related individuals such as parents or siblings? What about cousins or grandparents? How many times have we heard the comment, "Alice looks just like grandma Scott"? Where are the studies that corroborate the theory?

A third example relates to patterns observed in fires. The classic depth of char on wood indicating the time of fire development has been shown not to be true. This was easily disproven by analyzing, through experiments, that ventilation was a greater control factor for the depth of char on wood than the time of fire development neglecting the ventilation effects. Yet, experts still rely on depth of char analysis to locate the point of origin of a fire. These experts claim that depth of char on wood members indicates the length of time in fire development and thus the location of the fire origin. Another unproven fire contention is that travel wear patterns on carpeting will mimic accelerant wear patterns on the subfloor. This theory may or may not be true. Where are the tests? Fire investigators routinely see what appears to be pour patterns on floor surfaces. Normally, they would produce photographs and diagrams showing these patterns. They would then utilize a hydrocarbon detector to see if there were remnants of an accelerant. They may then take a sample for laboratory analysis for a particular accelerant. If an accelerant was found and could not be explained as occurring naturally, they may opine that it could have been used to accelerate the fire. That is the natural progression of the role of science in forensics. Such a progression fits the requirements of the scientific process but may not exclude other possibilities.

Natural forces produce devastating destruction that is measurable and quantifiable. Weather data in the United States is constantly monitored and measured by scientists. We know through weather services whether it is raining, snowing, hailing, or if the wind speed and direction are of a certain value that may cause destruction. The failure properties of materials are well known, understood, and quantified normally in the form of stress–strain curves for these materials. Human and animal tissue is also well understood and its failure points are known under a variety of ranges and conditions. Consequently, calculations can be made to determine if an event, such as a storm, produced a structural failure. Similarly, it can be calculated if a fall caused a closed head injury to a person. These processes are deeply rooted in science, can be quantified and repeated, and are consistent with the tenets of science.

We can summarize the role of science in forensics as follows. It is simply not sufficient for an investigator of forensic disciplines, to say, in my experience I have found that X, Y, and Z are true so that I may conclude Q. It is necessary to produce the underlying science, experimentation, and mathematical rigor to support the *conclusion*. The sum total of the data must be used in a scientific context. You cannot randomly exclude some of the data or evidence because it does not fit your theory. It is unethical to do so. In terms of uniqueness, that fact must be proven. Consider the following. Normal house fires produce temperatures of less than 2000°F. Often, we find melted metals or deflected steel that is sometimes attributed to the use of an accelerant. This contention cannot be proven without analyzing the effect of ventilation on the fire. Remember the old blacksmith who was simply melting iron or steel by the process of ventilation and reaching high temperatures. Today, we have tools such as diagnostic software called Fire Dynamics Simulation (FDS), developed by the National Institutes of Standards and Technology (NIST). With these tools, we can scientifically analyze the effects of accelerants and ventilation on fires. Such analysis is consistent with the role of science in forensics. These sophisticated computer tools have been tested and refined and are an aid in the analysis of fires, but they are not the sole authority. A variety of other technical tools and programs are available to aid the forensic investigator consistent with the scientific method. Again, we reiterate that these tools aid forensics but are not the sole method of analysis. All the evidence must conform to the conclusions that are derived from the particular forensic discipline.

In both the civil and the criminal environment, many forensic experts become advocates. They will support an alleged "theory" which only considers certain elements of the data and facts that support their conclusions. We will examine the role of the forensic expert in greater detail in a later chapter. It will become clear that neglecting some of the evidence or facts can readily lead to erroneous conclusions. Not only are those conclusions erroneous but often they are unethical.

4

The Need for Experimentation and Testing

The Confluence of Experiment and Theory

THE SCIENTIFIC METHOD

From a historical perspective, we need to go back approximately 2500 years to understand how the scientific method has evolved. Throughout the years there has been some disagreement concerning the approach that the scientific method should take in the development of scientific knowledge. Sad to say, and as the 2009 National Academy of Sciences Report has outlined, there is considerable disagreement in the area of forensics, as briefly described in Chapter 3. The main disagreement centers on the fact that many forensic disciplines do not follow the scientific method or skew their observations to fit a particular "theory" stated as proven "fact."

In ancient Greece, rational thinkers such as Democritus argued for a rational explanation of nature. Leucippus argued for the atom as a basis for all matter among other phenomenon that accounted for the observable universe. In fact, Democritus, a student of Leucippus, formulated and systematized the cosmological doctrines of his mentor. Democritus is famously known for his surviving fragmented works and treatises on ethics as well as the atomic concept of matter and of the void. The foundation of his perception of ethics was based on an ultimate good in which peace and tranquility are undisturbed by superstition or fear. Many scholars view the concepts of Democritus about nature and truth as the precursor of the scientific method. In his treatise *Metaphysics*, Aristotle stated that Democritus was of the opinion that "either there is no truth or to us at least it is not evident." A confounding statement to say the least.

In ancient India, rationalists such as Nyaya and Vaisesika disagreed with scholars such as Charvaka who argued for empiricism. Recall that empirical relates to the reliance on experiment or experience. In particular, Charvaka's thought was that when one infers a truth from observation, one must acknowledge some doubt. More clearly stated, inference is rejected to establish knowledge and truth. In more modern times, Rene Descartes advocated rationalism as a basis for scientific discovery, while Francis Bacon advocated empiricism and inductivism. A lasting legacy of Descartes is the metaphysical underpinnings of the Cartesian system which connects algebra and geometry and accounts for physical phenomenon in terms of mechanical systems. To Bacon, the natural sciences were split between *physics* and *metaphysics*. In his view, physics was an observable correlation and metaphysics was the mathematical construct that explains the regularities that we observe. Bacon saw mathematics as a logical means of expressing scientific observations.

In the modern era, the scientific method is characterized from the classical model developed by Aristotle. Aristotle developed the classic forms of reasoning based on abduction, analogy, deduction, and induction. It is wise to define these terms more closely. Abduction is the process of capturing, seizing, or carrying off. Analogy is a similarity in some manner or the inference that certain resemblances imply further similarity. Deduction is reasoning from the general to the specific, a conclusion reached by such reasoning. Induction is reasoning from particular facts to a general conclusion.

The emergence of a systematic process in science can be attributed to the period of enlightenment from the 1500s to the 1700s. During this period, a significant development in mathematics occurred with the introduction of functions, analytic geometry, calculus, and continuous mathematics and their application to science. Isaac Newton and Gottfried Leibnitz independently developed the basic tenets of differential and integral calculus. Calculus is simply a method or system of calculation or analysis using special symbolic notation.

The rapid development of mathematics during this period led to the emergence of what we now call the modern scientific method. This method is predicated on the melding of both classical methods of reasoning, that is rationalism and empiricism. To more closely describe the scientific method, we need to expand on its many components besides its historical development briefly described above.

The Oxford Dictionary defines the scientific method as a procedure or method consisting of systematic observation, measurement, experiment, formulation, testing, and modification of a hypothesis. It is based on empirical and measurable evidence consistent with recognized principles of logic and reasoning. A significant property of the method consists of empirical findings that are subject to falsification. Empirical findings indicate the reliance on experience and/or experiment. As it turns out, in the forensic sciences field, too much emphasis has been placed on the experience of the investigator in some of the fields discussed in this book. Not enough emphasis has been placed on the experimentation aspect of the alleged theory. Simply stated, many of these experience claims have not been subjected to falsification. That is, experiments have not been carried out to verify the hypothesis. Or, claims of experimental confirmation are alleged, never published or submitted for peer review. In some fields of the forensic sciences, the alleged peer review simply consists of like-minded individuals who support the underlying hypothesis. These groups strenuously support their disciples and wantonly attack anyone or any group who may disagree or question their hypothesis. Simply, by this method of entrenchment in their hypothesis, they violate the fundamental premise of the scientific method. That approach to forensic sciences is not science at all and leads to biases in their beliefs.

In order to adhere to the methods of science, a hypothesis must be tested in a controlled manner. A hypothesis becomes useful when it enables the user to predict outcomes, to correlate other data, and to apply reasoning to outcomes through deduction or through induction. This is readily performed in the forensic specialties of DNA, tool marks, fingerprints, electrical phenomenon, fire patterns, wind, and the laws of physics. However, in some of these areas, controlled testing has not been performed which has led to inaccurate, incorrect, and misleading beliefs and bias. It has promulgated false theories, conjectures, and opinions based on so-called experience, which is, in many cases, no more than bias. Properly designed experiments that are reproducible, peer reviewed, multifaceted, and verified by other investigators, diminish or curtail personal bias, circumstance, chance, and preference for a particular dogma. Note that the term dogmatic is an assertion without proof that is asserted positively and arrogantly. Junk science, more commonly described as pseudoscience, differs from true science in that it lacks a systematic characterization of the experiments or measurements. When true scientific measurements are carried out, they are quantified, tabulated, graphed, and mapped, and mathematical constructs are performed on the data to determine statistical properties. The error rate is established and any correlation or regression is noted and explained. Any measurements in science must also include the element of uncertainty. This uncertainty can be determined by repeated measurements and experiments. One set of data is not sufficient to verify a hypothesis. However, one negative result that does not fit the data may easily be sufficient to negate the hypothesis.

Once a hypothesis has been formulated, most probably through some observations or limited experimentation, significant emphasis needs to be placed on proving or disproving the hypothesis. This validation occurs in the form of extensive experiments and mathematical formulations to justify and corroborate the hypothesis. A properly formulated hypothesis is also predictive at best or is at least probabilistically accurate. More extensive testing of the hypothesis increases the probability of its robustness and assuredness that it is correct. In the absence of all of these caveats, the hypothesis is untestable and is therefore deemed unscientific and purely conjecture. A mathematically correct and scientific hypothesis is of sound reasoning, deductive, inductive, and predictive.

As outlined above, experimentation is a necessary but not a sufficient condition for the acceptance of a hypothesis. Testing may take many forms depending on the particular hypothesis and its application. The form of the tests must be well thought out, relevant, and include scientific apparatus in a laboratory setting or in the field, or involve multiple double-blind studies. These experiments and tests must be statistically significant. The experiments must be open, detailed, reproducible, and accountable, and welcome criticism from other observers and investigators.

Data sharing is an integral part of the scientific process. There are a plethora of venues to share data based on a hypothesis and the supporting experimentation. These venues include, but are not limited to, publication, presentation of papers and articles at conferences, discussions, and texts. Sharing with the scientific community allows for the evaluation of the hypothesis and encourages validation and, if necessary, any modifications to the hypothesis or of the experimentation protocols used to validate the results. It also allows for replication, acceptance, and confirmation within the scientific specialty. In rare cases, researchers make mistakes either during the hypothesis phase or during the experimental confirmation. Many of these mistakes are simply because "to err is human," but in other cases they are deliberate or produced by bias and blinders to recognized scientific procedures.

Some people attribute between one-third and one-half of scientific discoveries to luck or chance. This may be true for certain areas of endeavor in true basic science. By and large, chance discoveries in the forensic sciences do not seem to apply because forensics is an applied science that is not seeking fundamental truths. Aside from applying basic fundamental laws to an event, most forensic scientists and investigators are not revolutionizing basic science. They are, in fact, attempting to apply the basic principles of science to observed phenomenon. One exception in the forensic sciences is DNA. A possible reason for this exception in DNA analysis is that it was developed in a more fundamental scientific endeavor and later applied to forensics.

A classic example of a chance discovery is that of cosmic microwave background radiation. In 1964, Arno Penzias and Robert Wilson of Bell Telephone Laboratories constructed an antenna intended to be used for radio astronomy and satellite communication experiments. The antenna kept receiving a signal for which they essentially could not account. This signal turned out to be the cosmic microwave radiation predicted in 1948 by Ralph Alpher and Robert Herman as a result of the Big Bang. The Big Bang is now the recognized confirmation of the Standard Cosmological Model of the genesis of the universe.

MATHEMATICS

The role of mathematics in science cannot be overemphasized. As soon as civilization began, some formalism for keeping track was needed. Going back approximately 5000 years to Mesopotamia, Egypt, Assyria, Elba, and the entire Middle East region of the world where civilizations first began, a need for mathematics developed. This need was found in commerce, trade, and taxation as well as tracking the seasons for harvesting purposes. Knowledge of astronomy was paramount in keeping track of the time of the year.

The historical record between about 3000 BCE and 1800 BCE indicates that counting and measuring systems, multiplication, and division problems were solved. From 1800 BCE to about 900 BCE, the foundations of number systems, fractions, algebra, and decimal numbers were developed in the Middle East and China. Between 900 BCE and 400 BCE, the foundations of the Pythagorean Theorem were developed by Indian mathematicians.

The Greeks made most of the contributions to mathematics between 400 BCE and 300 CE, with some contributions from China, India, and the Mayan culture in the Americas. These contributions included the areas of trigonometry, matrices, geometry, solids, shapes, infinity, and the concept of zero. From 300 CE to about 1300 CE, Indian, Persian, Arabic, and Chinese scholars formulated methods to solve division by zero, solutions to quadric equations, the concepts of infinite series solutions, refinements to trigonometry, and solutions to higher-order functions.

During the period of the enlightenment, between 1300 CE and 1700 CE, European scholars developed the concepts of logarithms, solutions to higher-order equations, and Cartesian coordinates, and paved the way for the development of calculus which was produced by Newton and Leibniz independently.

Following the European tradition, Italian, French, English, German, Swiss, and Norwegian mathematicians dominated the further development of mathematics in the areas of topology, geometry, celestial mechanics, probability, and logic, and basic concepts of computational mechanics. These concepts developed and expanded from approximately 1700 to 1900. During the 20th century, further developments ensued in the areas of chaos theory, fractals, game theory, code theory, and number theory. Of course, these developments, mainly by European and American collaborators, led to the development of computers and sophisticated machines used in the forensic sciences. These computational mathematical methods have produced our modern understanding of the cosmos and our world.

This brief outline in the dual development of mathematics and science is just a rough entry into the development of these two disciplines. The reader is encouraged to seek further references in these critical areas to better understand the confluence of mathematics and the scientific method. It is critically important to refine forensic sciences to comport with the scientific method and address many of the issues that have arisen and have been addressed by many in the forensic community and the National Academy of Sciences in 2009. A deeper understanding of science and mathematics leads to more ethical practice in forensics where they may truly be classified as the *"forensic sciences."*

5

The Role of the Forensic Practitioner and Expert Witness

ROLE

A term that is often heard by some forensic practitioners is the *art and science* of a particular discipline. Let us be unambiguous and succinctly clear, art and science are two different and separate fields of study. Granted, science is beautiful, wonderous, exotic, artful, marvelous, exciting, awe-inspiring, and many more descriptive terms too numerous to mention. However, art is not science. Art is defined as human creativity, a skill or its application, a craft or its principles, or any branch of creative work. Products of art are paintings, sculptures, literature, and many others. It may refer to a branch of learning such as Liberal Arts. It may also mean wily, cunning, or a sly trick. How interesting is this latter part of the definition of art. Using Webster's definition, are we to infer that applying the term *"art and science"* to a particular forensic discipline means a form of deception by wile, cunning, or trick? Let us hope not. Unfortunately, in many instances that is exactly the case. Other terms associated with *art* are illustration, abstraction, imitation, modeling, description, portrayal, design, composition, performance, drama, poetry, fiction, singing, dancing, playing an instrument, personification, sketching, molding, shaping, painting, characterization, creating, sculpting, carving, etc. Some of these terms are common to science, such as modeling. However, in science, modeling has a distinctly different meaning as we will see.

Science is defined as systematized knowledge derived from observation, study, etc. It is a branch of knowledge which systematizes facts, principles, and methods. It may also be a skill or technique. It is an organized body of knowledge, department of learning, branch of knowledge, system of knowledge, body of fact, a highly developed skill, and ability. To be scientific is to be objectively accurate, precise, exact, clear, experimental, deductive, and methodically sound and logical. It is also descriptive with respect to its accuracy and error rates. It is recognized by its use of the terms theory and law that are physical and not subjective.

The term forensic is derived from the Greek forum or marketplace where debates are said to have taken place by the early philosophers of Rome and Greece. Forensic means of or suitable for public debate or argument. Specifically, it relates to the application of scientific knowledge to legal matters.

ROLE OF THE PRACTITIONER

Irrespective of the field of forensics, whether as an expert in DNA, geology, tool marks, fire sciences, ballistics, fingerprints, physics, accident reconstruction, or engineering, the practitioner needs to conform to some basic principles. What are these principles and norms? The principle or norm is the fundamental truth or law. It is a rule of conduct, its adherence to integrity, and the explanation of the scientific law relative to the method or natural action that is being testified to by the expert.

While carrying out these objectives or actions leading to a report, opinion, or testimony, the forensic expert must adhere to the following. First and foremost, the basic science must be established. Examples of the basic science are Newtonian mechanics, melting temperature of metals, reported and measured wind force at a particular time and location, vehicle crash tests, lightning activity, strength of materials, and many others. Many of these topics are derived from basic science, testing, data collection, and mathematics, and all must conform to the scientific method. They cannot be based on *"my experience and opinion."* Formulating the basic science for the expert's opinion, the practitioner must relay the testing that has been performed and substantiated by independent investigators. This independent testing will reveal any error rate or bias that may occur. The opinion of the expert must be based on all the available evidence. If some of the evidence does not conform to the opinion, it must be logically explained why it does not. It may be possible that during the data collection an error was made recording a number, or a miscalculation was made. Keep in mind that we are human and susceptible to making mistakes. With careful observations and analysis, most of these errors can be eliminated. However, it is unethical to simply disregard some of the data because it does not support the opinion of the expert. As an example, consider five measurements taken, of which three are deemed correct by the expert but two are not. The two that do not comport with the expert's opinion cannot simply be disregarded, there may be a slightly different opinion that is consistent with all the data. In fact, such omissions are common in accident reconstruction by both opposing experts and some law enforcement individuals. It is all too common to skew or disregard some of the evidence to fit a desired opinion or theory. Some of this inconsistent data may also be disregarded by the expert simply because it does not fit his opinion. There are areas in forensics that are replete with this total disregard for science and ethics. Guidelines for the role of the forensic practitioner may be found in the Federal Rules.

The Federal Rules of Evidence relative to the testimony of experts are as follows. First, we need to introduce a few basic definitions to more fully understand the role of the expert. These are described in Article VI—Witnesses. The rules recorded in this section are presented exactly as in the 2018 Federal Rules of Evidence.

Article VI—Witnesses

Rule 602. Need for Personal Knowledge

A witness may testify to a matter only if evidence is introduced sufficient to support a finding that the witness has personal knowledge of the matter. Evidence to prove personal knowledge may consist of the witness's own testimony. This rule does not apply to a witness's expert testimony.

Rule 607. Who May Impeach a Witness

Any Party, including the party that called the witness, may attack the witness's credibility.

Rule 608. A Witness

(a) **Reputation or Opinion Evidence.** A witness's credibility may be attacked or supported by testimony about the witness's reputation for having a character for truthfulness or untruthfulness, or by testimony in the form of an opinion about that character. But evidence of truthful character is admissible only after the witness's character for truthfulness has been attacked.

(b) **Specific Instances of Conduct.** Except for a criminal conviction under Rule 609, extrinsic evidence is not admissible to prove specific instances of a witness's conduct in order to attack or support the witness's character for truthfulness. But the court may, on cross-examination, allow them to be inquired into if they are probative of the character for truthfulness or untruthfulness of:
   (1) the witness; or
   (2) another witness whose character the witness being cross-examined has testified about.

By testifying on another matter, a witness does not waive any privilege against self-incrimination for testimony that relates only to the witness's character for truthfulness.

The next section, Rule 609. Impeachment by Evidence of a Criminal Conviction, is not covered by the authors because we strongly believe that convicted criminals should not serve as expert witnesses. Recall that the context of this book is on ethical behavior. Our opinion is that any person who has been convicted of criminal behavior is intrinsically not ethical. We stand by this opinion even if the witness, as an expert, has been rehabilitated, pardoned, the conviction annulled, or even if the president of the United States stipulated as such.

Rule 611. Mode and Order of Examining Witnesses and Presenting Evidence

(a) **Scope of Cross-Examination.** Cross-examination should not go beyond the subject matter of the direct examination and matters affecting the witness's credibility. The court may allow inquiry into additional matters as if on direct examination.

(b) **Leading Questions.** Leading questions should not be used on direct examination except as necessary to develop the witness's testimony. Ordinarily, the court should allow leading questions:

(1) on cross-examination; and
(2) when a party calls a hostile witness, an adverse party, or a witness identified with an adverse party.

Rule 612. Writing Used to Refresh a Witness

(a) **Scope.** This rule gives an adverse party certain options when a witness uses a writing to refresh memory:
  (1) while testifying; or
  (2) before testifying, if the court decides that justice requires the party to have those options.
(b) **Adverse Party's Options; Deleting Unrelated Matter.** Unless 18U.S.C. § 350 provides otherwise in a criminal case, an adverse party is entitled to have the writing produced at the hearing, to inspect it, to cross-examine the witness about it, and to introduce in evidence any portion that relates to the witness's testimony. If the producing party claims that the writing includes unrelated matter, the court must examine the writing in camera, delete any unrelated portions, and order that the rest be delivered to the adverse party. Any portion deleted over objection must be preserved for the record.
(c) **Failure to Produce or Deliver the Writing.** If a writing is not produced or is not delivered as ordered, the court may issue any appropriate order. But if the prosecution does not comply in a criminal case, the court must strike the witness testimony or—if justice so requires—declare a mistrial.

Rule 613. Witness

(a) **Showing or Disclosing the Statement During Examination.** When examining a witness about the witness's prior statement, a party need not show it or disclose its contents to the witness. But the party must, on request, show it or disclose its contents to an adverse party's attorney.
(b) **Extrinsic Evidence of a Prior Inconsistent Statement.** Extrinsic evidence of a witness's prior inconsistent statement is admissible only if the witness is given an opportunity to explain or deny the statement and the adverse party is given an opportunity to examine the witness about it, or if justice so requires. This subdivision (b) does not apply to an opposing party's statement under Rule 801(d)(2).

Rule 614. Court

(a) **Calling.** The court may call a witness on its own or at a party's request. Each party is entitled to cross-examine the witness.
(b) **Examining.** The court may examine a witness regardless of who calls the witness.
(c) **Objections.** A party may object to the court's calling or examining a witness either at that time or at the next opportunity when the jury is not present.

Rule 615. Excluding Witnesses

At a party's request, the court must order witnesses excluded so that they cannot hear other witnesses' testimony. Or the court may do so on its own. But this rule does not authorize excluding:

(a) a party who is a natural person;
(b) an officer or employee of a party that is not a natural person, after being designated as the party's representative by its attorney;
(c) a person whose presence a party shows to be essential to presenting the party's claim or defense; or
(d) a person authorized by statute to be present.

The preceding sections apply to all witnesses, and we emphasize that these should be clearly understood by all expert witnesses because in some instances, opposing attorneys will take advantage of the expert and attempt to trick the expert. An example of such a trick is when during cross-examination the opposing attorney will say words to the effect that in a prior trial or deposition you stated such and such. You may not recall the prior statement. At that time, you should request that the statement be produced. Of course, if they have such an impeachable statement, you have problems. If not, you can quickly disarm their trickery and shenanigans. Remember, you always have the right to explain your answers.

The sections we have outlined apply to all witnesses. Some of the sections have been disregarded as not pertinent for this treatise as explained. More significantly, Article VII relating to expert testimony is more directly applicable.

Article VII—Opinions and Expert Testimony

Rule 701. Opinion Testimony by Lay Witnesses

If a witness is not testifying as an expert, testimony in the form of an opinion is limited to one that is:

(a) rationally based on the witness's perception;
(b) helpful to clearly understanding the witness's testimony or to determine a fact in issue; and
(c) not based on scientific, technical, or other specialized knowledge within the scope of Rule 702.

Rule 702. Testimony by Expert Witnesses

A witness who is qualified as an expert by knowledge, skill, experience, training, or education may testify in the form of an opinion or otherwise if:

(a) the expert's scientific, technical, or other specialized knowledge will help the trier of fact to understand the evidence or to determine a fact in issue;
(b) the testimony is based on sufficient facts or data;
(c) the testimony is the product of reliable principles and methods; and
(d) the expert has reliably applied the principles and methods to the facts of the case.

Rule 703. Bases of an Expert

An expert may base an opinion on facts in the case that the expert has been made aware of or personally observed. If experts in the particular field would reasonably rely on those kinds of facts or data in forming an opinion on the subject, they need not be admissible for the opinion to be admitted. But if the facts or data would otherwise be inadmissible, the proponent of the opinion may disclose them to the jury only if their probative value in helping the jury evaluate the opinion substantially outweighs their prejudicial effect.

Rule 704. Opinion on an Ultimate Issue

(a) **In General—Not Automatically Objectionable.** An opinion is not objectionable just because it embraces an ultimate issue.
(b) **Exception.** In a criminal case, an expert witness must not state an opinion about whether the defendant did or did not have a mental state or condition that constitutes an element of the crime charged or of a defense. These matters are for the trier of facts alone.

Rule 705. Disclosing the Facts or Data Underlying an Expert

Unless the court orders otherwise, an expert may state an opinion—and give the reason for it—without first testifying to the underlying facts or data. But the expert may be required to disclose those facts or data on cross-examination.

Rule 706. Court-Appointed Expert Witnesses

(a) **Appointment Process.** On a party's motion or on its own, the court may order the parties to show cause why the expert witness should not be appointed and may ask the parties to submit nominations. The court may appoint any expert that the parties agree on and any of its choosing. But the court may only appoint someone who consents to act.

(b) **Expert's Role.** The court must inform the expert of the expert's duties. The court may do so in writing and have a copy filed with the clerk or may do so orally at a conference in which the parties have an opportunity to participate. The expert:
  (1) must advise the parties of any findings the expert makes;
  (2) may be deposed by any party;
  (3) may be called to testify by the court or any party; and
  (4) may be cross-examined by any party, including the party that called the expert.

(c) **Compensation.** The expert is entitled to a reasonable compensation, as set by the court. The compensation is payable as follows:
  (1) in a criminal case or in a civil case involving just compensation under the Fifth Amendment, from any funds that are provided by law; and
  (2) in any other civil case, by the parties in the proportion and at the time that the court directs—and the compensation is then charged like other costs.

(d) **Disclosing the Appointment to the Jury.** The court may authorize disclosure to the jury that the court appointed the expert.

(e) **Parties' Choice of Their Own Experts.** This rule does not limit a party in calling its own experts.

STATEMENTS

Many forensic investigators use statements as evidence to support their assertions. Statements are not scientific evidence and should never be used as such. As we have pointed out, once the science and the mathematical computations have been carried out, statements may be used to corroborate the evidence if they are in agreement. It should also be pointed out that some statements do not comport or agree with the scientific basis for the conclusions that are reached. The Federal Rules of Evidence define a "declarant" as the person who made a statement and that a "statement" is a person's oral assertion, written assertion, or non-verbal conduct meant as an assertion. Some statements are considered "hearsay." Hearsay means a statement that the declarant does not make and that is offered in evidence to prove the truth of the matter asserted in the statement.

There are many statements that are not hearsay, including federal statutes and those prescribed by the Supreme Court. There are also many exceptions to the rule against hearsay as detailed in Rule 803.

A final portion of the Federal Rules relates to evidence expressed as follows.

Article IX—Authentication and Identification

Rule 901. Authenticating or Identifying Evidence

(a) **In General.** To satisfy the requirement of authenticating or identifying an item of evidence, the proponent must produce evidence sufficient to support a finding that the item is what the proponent claims it is.

There are many examples of Rule 901 including distinctive characteristics, comparison by an expert, evidence about a process or system, and methods used in the analysis. Where applicable, the chain of custody must be clear and unbroken. This is usually carried out by a form that includes the following information.

Date received
Date transferred
Items listed and description of the evidence
Receiving agent
Transferring agent

STANDARDS

Introduction

During the years that the authors have been performing forensic investigations, it has become evident that there is a great need for standardization. The field of forensics is not well represented by a concise and exhaustive list of standards. Most of the standards that are available to the forensic practitioner are from technical societies associated with engineering disciplines, the federal government, the American Society of Testing and Materials (ASTM), and various private testing facilities. Fortunately, in most areas of forensic engineering, there is a wealth of information and standards that have been developed over the years. The main thrust of these standards is the same as that in engineering, to protect life and property.

In this book, the authors make no statement with regard to qualifications, experience, or determination as to the suitability of the experts. Simply, that is not the purview of the forensic practitioner. Forensic practitioners are not the gatekeepers of the system. It is not ethical for an expert to assess the suitability of another professional. The gatekeeper of the system is the judicial system. The court systems in this country have recognized experts in forensics from many backgrounds. The adversarial nature of the criminal and civil system is designed to challenge experts as to their suitability to offer opinions on such matters. Judges and juries determine the qualifications and competency of the experts. It should be recognized that the level of expertise required for these investigations varies with the complexity of the case. Many forensic investigations require only minimal mathematical skills and a rudimentary knowledge of the physical principles involved. It is recognized that many experts may be very well qualified by their experience and training although their traditional academic training may not be comparable. Some forms of analysis may require significant training in the physical sciences and mathematics that may be beyond the capabilities of some individuals including people with engineering and science degrees. This book is mainly geared toward the student or practitioner who is in a forensic sciences curriculum and illustrates the common methods in forensic failure and validation analysis.

The forensic student and practitioner should welcome standards and protocols because as humans we make mistakes. Standards and protocols keep us focused and on track. Protocols minimize mistakes and standards put us on a solid footing. Applying recognized standards to a forensic investigation makes our work and conclusions much easier and less subject to challenge. It is the method of science and should be embraced by all practitioners. Additionally, it conforms to ethical standards.

Protocol for Forensic Investigations

This section should not be construed to apply under all circumstances. Some of the material in this section is covered under the National Fire Protection Association (NFPA), Code of Federal Regulations (CFR), American Society of Civil Engineers (ASCE), American Institute of Chemical Engineers (AIChE), American Society of Mechanical Engineers (ASME), National Institute for Automotive Service Excellence (ASE), American Society of Metals (ASM), Society of Automotive Engineers (SAE), American National Standards Institute (ANSI), and ASTM standards and guidelines and may be considered repetitive. Most standards are now cross-referenced with the American National Standards Institute (ANSI). For example, the listing may say (ANSI/ASCE) to denote a cross-reference with the American Society of Civil Engineers. The cross reference may also be with a Code of Federal Regulations. Please refer to the applicable standards for your discipline for a more detailed explanation of procedural guidelines. Most forensic investigations require at least a fundamental knowledge of the applicable standards.

Standard Guide for Forensic Inspections and Investigations

Scope

This guide is for individuals who are investigating the events relating to incidents involving persons, vehicles, roadways, structures, equipment, materials, tools, firearms, or sites where a loss of property, injury, or a loss of life, criminal or civil event has occurred. The purpose of this guide is to provide a compendium of information and practices, but not to establish a standard practice or recommend a specific course of action. The guide is intended to increase the awareness of information and approach in this area. The guide covers methodologies and practices for the recognition, documentation, reporting, collection, and preservation of potentially relevant physical items and information pertaining to a forensic incident. It is also consistent with ethical standards and practices promulgated in this book.

This guide is intended to serve as a reference rather than as a definitive standard. As such, a forensic practitioner may use other relevant standards and protocols to supplement the information in this guide. The guide outlines many courses of action so that the investigator may choose the appropriate course of action relative to the investigation. The nature of the incident and the employer's requirements will also generally dictate the scope of work and practices required. For example, in some instances, the employer may require the investigator to work from existing evidence rather than collecting the evidence. Realizing that such restrictions tend to limit the scope and possibly the accuracy of the work, significant analysis can still be performed. Sometimes, the sites, buildings, structures, vehicles, or equipment may no longer be available or the site may have been altered. Under such circumstances, photographs, databases, simulations, and exemplars may be used to perform the analysis. Computer techniques may also be used to create a virtual scene based on measurements and photogrammetry.

Significance and Use

Every year, injuries, property damage, and business interruptions occur as a result of a variety incidents. The recording of information, physical data, and evidence following an incident is important if the origins and causes of an incident are to be determined. This document can help convey forensic findings to both technical and non-technical third parties. The documentary data, including reports and statements, is used to corroborate the findings.

Because the evidence at the scene of an incident is time-sensitive, forensic investigations conducted as soon as possible after the incident often collect the most useful information. In most instances, forensic practitioners are not afforded the privilege of investigating the incidents soon after they occur. Police or regulatory authorities investigate most incidents within minutes or hours. Police, fire departments, and other responding authorities having jurisdiction (AHJ) are required to document the incident scenes and often perform some of the most immediate site analysis and evidence collection. However, these authorities often have primary statutory responsibilities to protect life and property. Therefore, it is recognized that the reports generated by these agencies, while important, may not include all relevant data. It is in a follow-up role that private forensic practitioners play a vital role as they often have greater collection resources and more time to spend on the investigation than the responding AHJs.

Proper collection of incident details may allow for the replication or reconstruction of an incident. The reconstruction or replication of the incident may take many perfectly valid forms. The reconstruction of the incident, if warranted, can be performed by the application of basic physical laws. The reconstruction may be based on available data or on actual tests with exemplar structures or equipment. The reconstruction may be based on computer simulations and models. A combination of methods may be used to validate the results of the investigation and reconstruction. Wherever practical, it is suggested that more than one method of analysis be used to reach the conclusion of the forensic practitioner.

Equipment

Useful equipment for incident investigations and reconstructions include but are not limited to

(1) Measuring devices, total stations, transits, rolling tapes, measuring tapes, micrometers, calipers, dial indicators, feeler gauges, scales, pressure gauges, crush jigs, microscopes, investigative lights, etc.
(2) Diagnostic tools, data retrieval tools, volt-ohm meters, oscilloscopes, vacuum gauges, timing lights, calculators, computers, x-ray machines, MRIs, hardness testers, etc.
(3) SAE standard and metric wrenches and tools, jacks, stands, and equipment lifts.
(4) Mirrors, boroscopes, thermal imaging devices, microscopes, x-ray equipment, etc.
(5) Cameras with micro and macro capabilities, video and audio recorders.
(6) Maps, global positioning systems, aerial and satellite images.
(7) Incident reconstruction and simulation software, equipment specification databases, test data, drawing software.

Procedure

The procedure outlined below is not to be construed as a sequence of events that are to be followed in order of appearance. It is realized that these procedures will generally overlap, intersect, and follow in a random sequence.

(1) Historical and background data

Police reports, emergency responders reports, fire department reports, equipment repair estimates, police photographs, news coverage reports, photographs or video, adjuster photographs, injury or medical reports, witness statements, examinations under oath, depositions, maintenance records or repair records, weather and sun or moon position records, illumination records.

(2) On-site activities

Proper documentation of the site with measurements, photographs, or video; the use of exemplar equipment, actors, or vehicles to demonstrate particular characteristics concerning the events of the incident; studies relative to perception, visibility, illumination, and conspicuity.

(3) Machinery and equipment inspections

Establish protocols for the joint inspection of machines or equipment, or the retrieval of data from event recorders. Measurements with appropriate equipment along with photographs and video recordings should document the activities. Disassembly of components should be systematically documented. Destructive testing may be agreed upon.

(4) Post-site and post-equipment inspection activities

Interviews with police, emergency medical services (EMS), fire department personnel, repair or maintenance facilities, request for production of documents or evidence, aerial or satellite imagery, literature search, policies, codes, and standards, training records.

(5) Exemplars and testing

Useful information may be obtained from destructive and non-destructive testing of exemplar equipment or machinery. Such tests are often undertaken to determine the potential for or mode of failure or safety issues that may arise.

(6) Standard analysis

Basic physical laws, Newtonian mechanics, time motion analysis, damage analysis, mathematical modeling of events, photogrammetry, machinery or equipment performance characteristics, site or structure characteristics.

(7) Simulations and computer models

2D and 3D models and simulations utilizing commercial software.

(8) Research activities

Reports

Over the course of a forensic incident investigation and reconstruction, the forensic practitioner may be required to prepare multiple reports in various formats including but not limited to

(1) Verbal reports
(2) Status reports
(3) Preliminary reports
(4) Draft reports
(5) Interim reports
(6) Final reports
(7) Amendments to reports

The client may require the forensic investigation report to include, where applicable, the following information:

(1) Signature and professional licensing or certification stamps
(2) Credit given to any additional contributors
(3) Sources of data relied on and list of references and appendices
(4) Other reports, statements, or depositions used or referenced
(5) Drawings and calculations
(6) Opinions on origins and causes of the incident

6 Bias and Error

MISCONCEPTIONS

Over the past few years, much emphasis has been placed on errors in the forensic sciences. This emphasis has come about as a result of the 1993 Supreme Court Daubert decision, the Kumho Tire case, and the National Academy of Sciences Report in 2009, "Strengthening Forensic Science in the United States: A Path Forward." In this report, among other findings, two stand out with respect to the title of the chapter. These are

(1) The small amount of scientific research used to confirm the validity and reliability of forensic disciplines and established quantifiable measures of uncertainty in the conclusions of forensic analysis.
(2) The small number of research programs on human-observed bias and sources of human error in forensic examinations.

QUANTIFYING BIAS AND ERROR

This paucity, or incompleteness of data, or error, is often used to attack an expert in a manner that implies that data has either been skewed, disregarded, or falsified, or that the computations are outside of standard scientific methodology and are therefore erroneous. Although many of the criticisms are warranted, opposing attorneys have mischaracterized the rulings and the cases in order to attack the opposing expert. Many jurisdictions have now supplanted the Federal Rules of Evidence with Daubert-style hearings on the admissibility of the evidence provided by experts. One phalanx of attack is to claim that the computations are full of errors so that they fall outside of the recognized values or procedures. Another method of attack is to state that all possible variations and conditions have not been properly investigated. In some cases, experts claim that the subject matter in question is so complex that meaningful conclusions cannot be made. In other cases, with very limited testing, analysis, or statistically consistent results, a claim of a match is made. Both sides of the argument can be subject to bias, error, and ethical lapses. We see that type of attack on experts frequently in criminal as well as civil cases. When a suspect is apprehended and the evidence is very strong against that individual, the suspect may be arraigned, charged, and brought to trial. A typical defense includes allegations that all suspects were not excluded so that the suspect is wrongly accused. In other words, the investigating officers did not question all possible suspects whether they existed or not.

Consider the following example from a real case in a civil trial. A lady in a sedan claims that her vehicle was rear-ended by an SUV which then fled the scene. Inspection of the damage to her vehicle is not consistent with a rear-end collision. In fact, the damage is consistent with a sharp horizontal object being dropped on the trunk and rear bumper of the sedan. As a result of the alleged collision, the lady is claiming a multitude of ailments including diseased teeth requiring extraction and dental implants. The insurance company denies the claim because of the obvious discrepancies in the damage and the claimed injuries. Before trial, the attorney for the plaintiff makes a motion for a Daubert hearing to disqualify the expert because the expert did not include all vehicles ever made since the inception of the automobile. The expert did consider all SUVs but not, for example, a 1922 Cadillac. Notwithstanding the fact that SUVs have only been manufactured in the last couple of decades, and are outside the boundaries being claimed, the expert is not bound to consider data not relevant such as a Martian spaceship having caused the damage. Needless to say, the Daubert hearing did not disqualify the expert. Keep this in mind because a later example will further expound upon the arguments made.

ERROR

Before we begin the mathematical treatment of this chapter, we need to expand on the terms used to define the uncertainty in forensic calculations. We begin with error. Error is defined in the dictionary and in people's minds as a mistake, inaccuracy, miscalculation, blunder, or oversight. It is the state or condition of being wrong in conduct or judgment. An argument is generally made that the techniques, equations, data, or some other form of analysis are incorrect or outside of the realm of accepted practice. When error or error rate is calculated or implied in the sciences, it has a totally different meaning. Consider the following:

Statistical error is not a mistake but rather the difference between the computed, measured, or estimated value and the actual value.

In mechanics when a system of the form $\mathbf{Ax} = \mathbf{b}$ *is solved, there is a difference in the inaccuracy in* $\mathbf{x}$ *and the residual, the inaccuracy in* $\mathbf{Ax}$.

In mathematics, error is the difference between an actual value and the estimated or computed value. Error also means the difference between the actual value and the truncated value where only the first few terms of an infinite series are used.

A better description of error is then the uncertainty in the computation or assessment of the values used in the computation. In nature, many parameters vary within some specified range. As an example, the strength of bone is known within a range of values, which does not mean that when performing a calculation on a bony structure, we may substitute any value for its strength or utilize a value outside of the known range of the parameter. Therefore, it is better to state the variability of the parameter within the known uncertainty and perform the calculations accordingly. Simply put, we should give the range of values that include the uncertainty and the variability.

The arguments posed above lead to another term called sensitivity. In our mathematical formulation of the models that we use to describe an effect (the equations we use to make the computations), some parameters that vary will have a great effect on the outcome. Others may not affect the computations as much or maybe not at all. This analysis or measure is what we call sensitivity.

When being cross-examined, it behooves the forensic practitioner to clearly and succinctly explain what is meant by error in a scientific or mathematical context. It is best to answer in terms of sensitivity, uncertainty, and probability instead of error so as to clarify the concepts for the judge and the jury. Assuming that the computations have been carried out correctly, when asked to state the error, it is much more descriptive to say that there is no error but there is variability and uncertainty within certain bounds dictated by the known scientific literature and the scientific method. By performing a variety of computations for all the variables that are sensitive in the equations, and those that are not, the essential constituents are analyzed. It is very helpful to graph or plot the results as these make strong demonstrative evidence in the courtroom or in a deposition. Many of the terms in an equation may not be subject to change as they could be constants such as the acceleration of gravity. In general, most equations in science may be functions of several variables.

Sensitivity

In general, an equation dependent on n variables can be expressed as

$$P = f\left(x_1, x_2, \ldots, x_n\right) \tag{6.1}$$

First, let us consider the case where an equation is a function of only one variable $P = f(x)$.

The sensitivity of P to the variable x is defined as

$$S_x^P = \lim_{\Delta x \to 0} \frac{\frac{\Delta P}{P}}{\frac{\Delta x}{x}} = \frac{x}{P} \lim_{\Delta x \to 0} \frac{\Delta P}{\Delta x} = \frac{x}{P}\frac{\partial P}{\partial x} = \frac{\partial(\ln P)}{\partial(\ln x)} \tag{6.2}$$

Applying the basic definition of sensitivity, the following relationships may be developed:

$$S_x^{cx} = 1 : c = \text{constant} \tag{6.3}$$

$$S_x^P = -S_x^{\frac{1}{P}} \tag{6.4}$$

$$S_x^P = -S_{\frac{1}{x}}^P \tag{6.5}$$

$$S_x^{P1P2} = S_x^{P1} + S_x^{P2} \tag{6.6}$$

$$S_x^{\frac{P1}{P2}} = S_x^{P1} - S_x^{P2} \tag{6.7}$$

$$S^P_{x^n} = \frac{1}{n} S^P_x \tag{6.8}$$

$$S_x^{P1+P2} = \frac{P1 S_x^{P1}}{P1+P2} + \frac{P2 S_x^{P2}}{P1+P2} \tag{6.9}$$

Since most functions are in terms of various parameters, it is important to determine the parameter deviations. To do so, we begin with the basic definition as expressed in Equation 6.2. For small deviations in x, we can determine the change in the function due to one element as

$$\nabla P \cong S_x^P \frac{\Delta x}{x} P \tag{6.10}$$

For multiple elements, we may expand Equation 6.9 in a Taylor series to obtain

$$\Delta P \cong \frac{\partial P}{\partial x_1}\Delta x_1 + \frac{\partial P}{\partial x_2}\Delta x_2 + \cdots + \frac{\partial P}{\partial x_m}\Delta x_m + \text{higher-order terms} \tag{6.11}$$

For small variations in Δx_j, we neglect the higher-order terms so that

$$\Delta P \cong \sum_{x_j}^{m} \frac{\partial P}{\partial x_j}\Delta x_j = \sum_{x_j}^{m}\left[\frac{\partial P}{\partial x_j}\right]\left[\frac{x_j}{P}\right]\left[\frac{\Delta x_j}{x_j}\right] P = \sum_{x_j}^{m} S^P_{x_j} V_{x_j} \tag{6.12}$$

where $V_{x_j} = \Delta x_j / x_j$ is the per unit change in the parameter x and is known as the variability of x.

For example, a simple but quite accurate approximation for the tensile stress on a human vertebra is given by

$$\sigma_s \cong \frac{0.003 w_T}{ndA} v^2 \tag{6.13}$$

where

- n = number of vertebrae
- d = distance from the lower spine to the rest of the spine (approximately 0.2 feet)
- A = cross-sectional area on the spine (approximately 660 mm²)
- w_T = weight of the individual in pounds
- v = speed of impact (in feet per second)

Applying Equation 6.7 to Equation 6.12, we find the following sensitivities:

$$S^{\sigma_s}_{w_T} = 1; S^{\sigma_s}_{v} = 2; S^{\sigma_s}_{n} = S^{\sigma_s}_{d} = S^{\sigma_s}_{A} = -1 \tag{6.14}$$

$$\frac{\Delta\sigma_s}{\sigma_s} = S_{w_T}^{\sigma_s}\left[\frac{\Delta w_T}{w_T}\right] + S_v^{\sigma_s}\left[\frac{\Delta v}{v}\right] + S_n^{\sigma_s}\left[\frac{\Delta n}{n}\right] + S_d^{\sigma_s}\left[\frac{\Delta d}{d}\right] + S_A^{\sigma_s}\left[\frac{\Delta A}{A}\right] \quad (6.15)$$

$$\frac{\Delta\sigma_S}{\sigma_S} = \frac{\Delta w_T}{w_T} + \frac{2\Delta v}{v} - \frac{\Delta n}{n} - \frac{\Delta d}{d} - \frac{\Delta A}{A} \quad (6.16)$$

It is interesting to note that if all the parameters above vary by 10%, the tensile stress on the vertebrae does not change at all. This example shows how variability in one parameter may counteract the variability in another parameter. This example also shows how we may approach the variation in a calculation to show how a particular parameter affects the outcome of the calculation. For example, if we just consider the variation in the velocity of Equation 6.13 and let the velocity change from say 5 to 6 miles per hour, a change of 20%, the change in the stress varies by an increasing factor of two. The stress equation is very sensitive to speed but not as sensitive to the other parameters. It also demonstrates the non-linearity of the equations that describe the tensile stress of the spine. A very critical factor in some instances, but not necessarily in others. To summarize this concept, the forensic expert should be critically aware of these variations in the associated parameters, and be able to succinctly describe their effect.

PROBABILITY

As in all of science, when performing calculations, it becomes necessary to perform some statistical computations. For example, if the calculations are for the probability of matching the lands and grooves of a bullet to a particular firearm, it is simply not sufficient to match one striation. The lands and grooves around the entire circumference of the bullet must be matched. Otherwise the match does not exist. Furthermore, it is critical to perform a statistically valid comparison to many identical weapons in order to scientifically prove the assertion that the bullet in question was fired from an individual gun. Simple tests by the authors on tool marks created by guns clearly dispute the assertion that individuality and uniqueness exist in this field. The computations are always based on a central measure of the parameter in question and are defined in this section. If we assume that the range of events varies from 1 to n so that for every value of x, there is a descriptive term $f_i \geq 0$. This descriptive term may be the frequency, the mass, the stress, the probability, or even the reliability of the occurrence of the event. The total weight is the sum of all the possibilities or

$$N = \sum_{i}^{m} f_i \tag{6.17}$$

The arithmetic mean is

$$x_{am} = \sum_{i}^{m} \frac{f_i x_i}{N} \tag{6.18}$$

The geometric mean is

$$x_{gm} = \left[\prod_{i}^{m} x_i^{f_i} \right]^{\frac{1}{N}} \tag{6.19}$$

The mode, M_o, for unweighted terms ($x_1, \ldots, x_N$) is the value about which x_i most densely clusters. The median, M_e, for unweighted terms is the value equal to or exceeded by exactly half of the values x_i. The root mean square is given by

$$\text{RMS} = \sqrt{\frac{\sum_{i}^{N} \left[f_i x_i^2 \right]}{N}} \tag{6.20}$$

The standard deviation is

$$sd = \sqrt{\frac{\sum_{i}^{N} \left[x_i - x_m \right]^2}{N}} \tag{6.21}$$

The variance is

$$V = \left[sd \right]^2 \tag{6.22}$$

The probability that an event E will occur is given by

$$\text{P}(\text{E}) = \frac{m}{n} \tag{6.23}$$

where

E is the event
P(E) is the probability that the event will occur
m is the corresponding event
n is the number of ways possible

If we consider two events, A and B, the following relations hold true:

P(A) = probability of event A
P(B) = probability of event B

$P(A')$ = probability that event A does not occur
$P(A/B)$ = conditional probability of event B, given event A
$P(A \cup B)$ = probability that event A and or event B occurs. Union.
$P(A \cap B)$ = probability that event A and event B both occur. Intersection.

$$P(A \cap B) = P(A)P(B) \tag{6.24}$$

A term that is loosely thrown around in many of the so-called forensic sciences is *"individuality"* or *"uniqueness."* The alleged meaning of the term relates to a variety of disciplines such as *tooth marks, tool marks, fingerprints, lands and grooves,* and *firing pin impressions*. The allegation is that the imprint marks made by these various items are unique. It is questionable and suspect that these imprints are, in fact, unique. There are no detailed scientific or robust studies from a statistical framework for these allegations to be true. For example, a stab wound may be consistent with a brand X, model Y butcher knife that is mass produced, but could it be item 20001 or 20003? Who can tell if they are identically forged and stamped? To be certain, the experienced machinist who produced the items could not differentiate between the two. How then could a so-called tool mark expert with no machinist experience who has no clue of tolerances or machine practices be able to distinguish and identify the item in question?

7

Ethics

INTRODUCTION

In a broader sense, we need to establish some common aspects of ethical behavior in the forensic sciences. We need to distinguish between necessity and sufficiency in the practice of the particular forensic field. Necessity and sufficiency are not mutually exclusive. By this, we mean that it is not just necessary to have experience in a particular field and it is also not just sufficient to have this experience. Both are important. The experience must be based on the fundamental principles of science and mathematics. It must consort with recognized tests, experiments, theoretical underpinnings, and validation studies. The error rate and bias must be computed and expounded on. Without these caveats, the opinions of the proponent are not science, and without these proper rigors dictated by the scientific method, they cannot be characterized as science.

The broad category of the alleged forensic sciences includes tool marks, tire marks, fingerprints, foot impressions, teeth marks, and handwriting analysis. These types of impression markings are predicated on an unproven theory of uniqueness, which is referred to as the *Theory of Discernible Uniqueness*. The claim of uniqueness in forensic fields has no basis in science and has been dismissed as completely unwarranted. It is also unethical to claim that uniqueness exists in the forensic fields because it is readily disproven. In these fields, there is insufficient evidence and data to correctly and scientifically attribute a probability that the patterns match a particular impression subject or object. These fields of forensic science are diametrically opposed to a field such as physics for example. In physics, if we drop an object from a height of say 10 meters, we know the outcome because we have never observed any other path or direction that the object may take. It falls to the ground. It can be described mathematically and can be experimentally proven time after time. In fact, we can accurately describe the motion and the attraction of gravity in other celestial bodies such as the moon. To our human knowledge, it has never been disproven so we can summarize it as a law of physics. Recall our discussion of the difference and the similarity between a theory and a law in science in previous chapters. The supposition of *discernible uniqueness* cannot be classified as a theory, much less as a law. The main reason that it cannot be classified as such is because there is insufficient or non-existent data to do so. It is simply an incorrect non-scientific conjecture.

IN ENGINEERING

Engineering is highly regulated at the state and national level. Each state has a Board of Professional Engineering. At the national level, the rules are promulgated by the National Society of Professional Engineers (NSPE). Under the preamble of the NSPE Code, it states that "Engineers must perform under a standard of professional behavior that requires adherence to the highest principles of ethical conduct." As part of their professional obligation, the NSPE Code requires that engineers shall avoid all conduct or practice that deceives the public. Specifically, they shall avoid the use of statements containing a material representation of fact or omitting a material fact. Recall that in a legal sense, the word "shall" is mandatory or, if the reader wishes, obligatory. There is no wiggle room with the word shall. In all United States codes and regulations, whether state, federal, or specific as a national standard, the word "shall" indicates a mandatory requirement.

Thus, from an engineering perspective, if an expert chooses to disregard pertinent data because that data does not fit his or her theory and conclusions, then he or she is being unethical. For example, let us consider a case where an engineer is hired to perform an accident reconstruction years after the incident. The case involves a pedestrian who was struck by a vehicle. The police department measured the site including the location of the point of impact of the vehicle with the pedestrian who was struck. Based on this impact location, they further measured the location of the right and left shoes that were dislodged from the pedestrian on impact and the location of the body at its rest position. The rest position of the vehicle was also measured based on the impact point. However, in their reconstruction, the expert simply moved the vehicle–pedestrian impact point to a different location based on no data. The impact point was apparently moved to fit their scenario or "theory" of the collision to exacerbate the involvement of the pedestrian. This scenario is clearly unethical because material facts are being omitted. The relative positions of the shoes, the body on impact and at rest, and the rest position of the striking vehicle are all interrelated. Simply moving the impact point changes all the dynamics of the reconstruction. Clearly, ethical standards would not be adhered to in this case. Sadly, this type of malfeasance occurs too often. Physical data or evidence simply cannot be disregarded.

IN FINGERPRINT ANALYSIS

There are about seven billion people in the world. Let us restrict that number to the United States and limit the number of people to three hundred million. In a large city, we may consider one million people. Out of that million, just consider adults between the ages of 20 and 50, dropping the estimate to 200,000 people. Now, just consider men and you come up with 100,000 eligible men who might be suspect. Of those, say that 1% have a propensity for a criminal act and you end up with a possibility of 1000 men. At this point, let us assume an unproven fact that fingerprints are truly unique.

Let us now muddy the waters even further. At a crime scene, the perpetrator who leaves finger, hand, or foot impressions does not do so in the elegant manner that prints are obtained when a person is fingerprinted by carefully rolling the impression on a nice clean white card. The prints at a scene are generally latent or partial. Latent simply means that they are not normally visible to the naked eye. In a forensic sense, the latent term for a fingerprint implies that the friction ridge impression was deposited accidentally or by chance. A partial print contains only a portion of the entire ridge structure of the particular body part. An additional complication is introduced at the crime scene because the motion of the perpetrator will alter the pattern in innumerable ways. These alterations due to translation, rotation, and impact pressure tend to distort the flexible skin of the friction ridge. In fact, it is well known that no two fingerprints are exactly alike from the same individual recorded immediately after each other in a controlled environment. Given this well-documented variability, is it ethical to claim with certainty that the latent fingerprint belongs to a particular individual? Another consideration is the fact that only certain points are considered when an examiner is making a determination. Fingerprint analysis is a subjective determination by the analyst. Essentially, the examiner chooses the features that are compared. As the National Academy of Sciences has stated, fingerprint analysis can be a likely tool in the courts, but it is simply not true that it has no error.

HANDWRITING

This is an area that experts have long claimed to be essentially infallible. The experts will take a small portion of the writing, such as the direction of a stroke on a particular letter, to claim that it is consistent with a particular individual. For example, most people when writing the lower case "g" will stroke in a downward direction after counterclockwise rounding the top of the letter and then clockwise rounding the bottom of the letter. However, many people may not follow these particular strokes while forming a "g." We have all seen such examples that point to impostors being caught when they fake other's handwriting in popular crime shows. Is there any scientific basis for such assumptions?

Some handwriting experts refer to themselves as "graphologists." "Graphoanalysis" is an offshoot of graphology which maintains that sweeping physical and psychological diagnoses can be made based on the examination of letter shapes. Some of the claims also consist of emotions based on whether the writer slants the letters to the right or to the left. The claim is that slanting the letters leftward, the individual is withdrawn, to the right the writer is carried away by their feelings. If the writing slant varies from right to left, the writer is untruthful or stressed out. Where this analysis arises from is truly unknown. What types of tests have been conducted to make this assertion? None are cited in the known literature. Did someone line up clinically depressed individuals en masse and analyze their writing? Was the same test administered to jubilant individuals? Did these folks write with the left hand or the right hand? Was that significant? So many questions and no science-based answers.

The primary basis for the area of handwriting analysis is the forensic document examination of a questioned document. It is based on the scientifically unproven theory that every person in the world has a *unique* way of writing. This uniqueness theory, which appears in several fields of study, is simply not proven to any degree of scientific scrutiny.

A famous case of the shortcomings of handwriting analysis is that of "the lost Hitler diaries." This case points out that a good simulation of a writing sample can be undetectable. Although a team of recognized document examiners all concluded that the diaries were written by the same person who wrote the exemplars, they were not written by Hitler. This fact was proven by the analysis of the paper and the ink, in that the paper on which the lost diaries were written was not produced until 1954. Only about 10 years after his death, but a minor burp on the theory! Additionally, the ink used was approximately 12 months old. Ironically, the same person who wrote the exemplars also wrote the diaries. However, it was not Adolf Hitler.

There are many examples of incorrect testimony by handwriting experts claiming that the likelihood of a sample they examined matched a particular person to the exclusion of all others. In order to scientifically state ethically that the identification was determined within acceptable statistical parameters, there should be a concrete set of guidelines and calculations that are followed. We do not propose to formulate these guidelines and calculations simply because in our experience, we both write in different ways as a regular course. Sometimes our writing slants forward, vertically, or rearward. Analyze all the writing styles of a particular person and our bet is that you may come up with two or three different individuals, or maybe more. Some people have a systematic and non-changing style of writing. Others vary their style for a variety of reasons or simply on a whim.

From a logical, scientific perspective, a handwriting examiner who looks at two or three examples of a person's handwriting and comes up with a conclusion cannot say it is science. This is true because the samples are very limited and do not represent the totality of the evidence. It is paramount to taking three data points from thousands and coming up with a conclusion. Just not science.

TOOL MARKS

The most widely reported misuse of this dubious so-called science is in the identification of bullets and their casings. Secondly, other items such as knives and screwdrivers are said to be unique. Let us look at one instance. Consider two identically manufactured Brand X screwdrivers that were produced sequentially. The allegation is that each of these two screwdrivers will produce distinguishable marks unique to each. What a preposterous allegation! Any person with experience in a machine shop knows this to be malarkey. The question arises, where are the double-blind studies to corroborate this allegation? This so-called "tool mark evidence" is often used to compare striations on bullet fragments called lands and grooves, firing pin and ejection marks on bullet casings, the use of a bolt cutter on a padlock, a hammer blow impact, or any number of tool impressions that these examiners look at. These protagonists allege that the manufacturing processes used to make the tools create unique imperfections on the tool surfaces, and that uniqueness is reflected in the tool marks created when the tools are used. In general, tool mark examiners have no experience with machining processes, the tolerances of those processes, little experience with dynamical forces, or solid data to back up their contentions.

SHOES AND TIRE MARKS

We concede that two Nike size eight shoes will have sole patterns that are indistinguishable when new. The same is true for two Pirelli model XYZ tires and it can be said that the imprints examined are a match. However, tool examiners go beyond and attest that the wear marks are exclusive to an individual or a vehicle. How can such an allegation be made without knowing the entire history of the item? Such evidence is unknown so that the imprint identification again leads to ethical issues when the examiner alleges that they have a unique match. Also, a conundrum arises because of the alleged theory of uniqueness. How can the manufacturing process produce unique marks on each and every item made and these marks not alter the wear patterns of the item? For example, the rubber composition of a particular sole is not homogeneous and deposited on the left side of the sole of 200 shoes. This inhomogeneity causes a significant wear pattern on the left side of all these shoes. Can we say that the wear patterns are unique to an individual?

BITE MARKS

How about genetics? One of us had a father with crooked teeth. Additionally, the father had a granddaughter with the same crooked teeth until they were corrected with braces. How often do we see similarities in families and sometimes between strangers? If you believe in evolution, and we do, we have evolved from a common ancestor who lived more than 500 million years ago and who did not look anything like us. Can the genetic code produce similar or almost identical features on unrelated individuals? Seems very likely and worthy of some serious scientific investigation.

As humans, we are all related, so that many traits are common to all of us. Another troubling allegation to bite mark identification stems from the fact that impressions taken at the dental offices of the suspected perpetrator are carefully controlled. During a violent attack that produces a bite mark, such a controlled *environment does not exist and cannot be reproduced.* Consequently, it seems unethical that the examiner would take the leap and claim a match because the dynamic forces in the attack are unknown and would influence the bite impressions.

In 2009, the National Academy of Sciences published its report "Strengthening Forensic Science in the United States: A Path Forward." This document lists 13 recommendations. Pertinent to this topic on ethics, they state the following:

Recommendation 9:

> *The National Institute of Forensic Science (NIFS), in consultation with its advisory board, should establish a national code of ethics for all forensic science disciplines and encourage individual societies to incorporate this national code as part of their professional code of ethics. Additionally, NIFS should explore mechanisms of enforcement for those forensic scientists who commit serious ethical violations. Such a code should be enforced through a certification process for forensic scientists.*

They further expand on this topic by stating that the practices of the forensic scientists be based on education consistent with validated scientific principles. They specify that part of the training must be based on the scientific area in question and that it includes calculations along with statistics and probability.

8

The Court System and the Role of the Attorney

Limitations Placed on the Expert

Sometimes, attorneys will stifle an expert for a variety of reasons. Most of the time there are legitimate reasons to limit the testimony of an expert. In many instances, the court itself will limit the expert testimony. In this chapter, we explore some of the pitfalls from an ethical standpoint that may occur when there is a failure to succinctly communicate the activities of the expert. Although we have essentially paraphrased the rules under federal guidelines, state and civil procedure rules do not significantly differ. As an expert, it is important to be aware of the general rules of court procedures because they will instruct the expert on the limitations that may arise in a particular case. These limitations will also guide the expert in his methodology and preparation in the case and at trial. Typically, the expert should assume that any case he works on is subject to go to trial. Realistically, although a small percentage will get to the deposition stage, a much smaller percentage will go to trial.

RULES OF EVIDENCE

Under Rule 16, Discovery and Inspection, of the Federal Rules of Criminal Procedure, both the government and the defendant or, in civil cases, the plaintiff and the defendant, have a duty to disclose. In particular, reports of examinations and tests performed by the government/plaintiff must be made available by the government/plaintiff to the defendant. Additionally, a written summary of any testimony that the government intends to use under Rules 702, 703, or 705 of the Federal Rules of Evidence must be provided.

Similarly, the defendant has a duty to disclose any evidence that the defendant intends to use in their case-in-chief at trial. Disclosure of reports and scientific tests or experiments must be provided as well as any expert witnesses who may be called to testify. If either party discovers additional evidence before or during the trial, the evidence must be promptly disclosed.

Under the Federal Rules of Civil Procedure, the regulations pertaining to disclosures and discovery are a little more detailed. Rule 26 details some of the procedure that is to be followed. In general, initial disclosures must be made at or within 14 days after the Rule 26(f) conference which sets the Planning for Discovery. A party is not excused from making its disclosures because it has not fully investigated the case or because it challenges the sufficiency of another party's disclosure or because another party has not made its disclosure.

One of us has experienced this conundrum. The opposing party did not disclose diagrams to be used at trial until the night before the testimony of their expert. The defense attorney did not object to the late disclosure of this evidence. The judge allowed these diagrams to be entered at trial. The defense attorney for our side thought he would punish the plaintiff's attorney by submitting our diagrams to the opposition at 11.30 p.m. before our testimony. The next day at trial, the plaintiff's attorney objected to our diagrams, successfully stating that they did not have sufficient time to examine the diagrams. So much for the argument that my hands are bigger than yours! What should have occurred is that the defense attorney should have at least objected to the late introduction of the plaintiff's diagrams, but more importantly submitted our diagrams in a timely manner because they were in his possession six weeks before trial. Ethical standards require us to follow the rules whether the opposition does or not. In this particular case, our diagrams, based on incongruous, incontestable, and incontrovertible physical facts, would have contradicted the plaintiff's expert's false assertions of the location of critical evidence. In that case, both attorneys failed to follow ethical norms, which may have altered the outcome of the trial. Additionally, the plaintiff's expert was not ethical in that he fabricated evidence.

The following rules should always be adhered to in any case because they are designed to keep the playing field fair. Study these so that you are familiar with general procedures.

Under Rule 26 (2) *Disclosure of Expert Testimony.*

(a) **In General.** In addition to the disclosures required by Rule 26, a party must disclose to the other parties the identity of any expert witness it may use at trial to present the evidence under Federal Rule of Evidence 702, 703, or 705.

(b) **Witnesses Who Must Provide a Written Report.** Generally unless otherwise stipulated or ordered by the court, the disclosure of the witness must be accompanied by a written report, which is prepared, written, and signed by the witness.

More specifically, if the witness is one retained or employed to provide expert testimony in the case or one whose duties as the party's employee regularly involve giving expert testimony, more stringent constraints are placed on the expert. Specifically, the report must contain the following:

(1) A complete statement of all opinions the witness will express and the basis and reason for them.
(2) The facts or data considered by the witness in forming the opinions.
(3) Any and all exhibits that will be used to summarize or support the facts and opinions.
(4) The qualifications of the witness including a listing of all publications by the witness in the past 10 years.
(5) A listing of all the other cases for the preceding 4 years where the expert has testified in a deposition or at trial.
(6) The compensation paid to the witness for the analysis, calculations, opinions, and report in the case being testified.

(c) **Certain Witnesses May Not Provide a Written Report.** The court may rule that the witnesses need not provide a written report if the following conditions are met.

(1) The subject matter about which the expert witness is expected to present evidence under Federal Rules of Evidence 702, 703, 705; and

(2) A summary of the facts and opinions about which the expert witness is expected to testify.

(d) **Time to Disclose Expert Testimony**. A party must make the disclosures at the times and in the sequence that is ordered by the court. If the court does not stipulate the time and the sequence of the disclosure, they must be made:

(1) At least 90 days before the date set for trial or for the case to be ready for trial; or

(2) If the evidence is intended solely to contradict or rebut evidence on the same subject matter identified by another party within 30 days after the other party's disclosure.

In the case we discussed above, it is clear that both sides of the argument were not following regular orderly procedure. Since the case was in a State District Court, the rules may not have been exactly as we have outlined for the Federal Rules; nonetheless, there would have been a set itinerary for discovery and disclosures.

In general, unless the court limits discovery, the scope of discovery is as follows. Both parties may obtain discovery regarding non-privileged matter that is relevant to either party's claim. The court may alter the rules by limiting the number and the extent of depositions or requests. Further limitations may be placed on electronically stored information if the information is not reasonably accessible due to undue burden or cost. The court may also limit discovery if it deems it to be cumulative or duplicative, or it may be obtained from other sources which may be less expensive, more convenient, and less burdensome to the other party. Limits may also be placed if the party seeking discovery has sufficient time to obtain the information or if it is outside the scope permitted by the rules.

TRIAL PREPARATION OF EXPERTS

The opposing party in litigation may depose the person identified as an expert and whose opinions may be presented at trial. Under Rule 26, a report is required from the expert. The deposition is generally conducted only after the report submitted to the opposing party is reviewed and analyzed by their expert or experts. In complex litigation, one or both parties may employ a variety of experts to attempt to discredit the opposing party's expert.

There are several protections for trial preparation. Draft reports and disclosures are generally protected under Rule 26 regardless of the form in which the draft is recorded. Additionally, any communication between the attorney and the expert is protected regardless of the form of the communication. There are some exceptions to this protection. These are the compensation provided to the expert, the facts and data that the expert's attorney provided and were used in the formulation of the expert's opinion, and any identifying assumptions that the attorney provided and that the expert relied on in forming an opinion to be expressed at trial.

Some experts are retained by either party but are never intended to be deposed or to testify at trial. These experts are used for trial preparation in an attempt to discover pertinent facts about the case which may bolster their theories of the case or, more generally, to expose weaknesses in the case. Remember, the role of the attorney is not necessarily to reveal all the facts but to represent their client in their best manner within the rules of law. Contrary to the attorney's role, the expert's role is to reveal the facts whether they support or degrade the side they represent. Naturally, if the expert's opinions do not align with the particular side that hired them, they most likely will not be used at trial but may aid in discovering pertinent weaknesses inherent to their case of which the attorney needs to be aware.

There are a couple of exceptions to this rule in the case of Physical and Mental Examinations under Federal Rule 35 or by showing exceptional circumstances where it would not be practical for the party to obtain the facts or opinions by other means. This last exception is very difficult to assert in the fact- and data-driven context of this book.

FEES

Whether the expert is retained by either side and unless manifest injustice would result, the court requires that the party seeking discovery pay the expert reasonable fees for the time spent in responding to discovery under Rule 26 and the expenses incurred reasonably in obtaining the facts and opinions of the expert.

From an ethical standpoint, it is necessary to point out a caveat emptor (let the buyer beware) into which the opposing attorney should be forced. The rule is clear, if the expert spends time preparing for the deposition, a part of the response to the discovery, the expert is to be compensated. Most experts are not aware of this rule. Consequently, the opposing attorney will deny payment for any preparation for the deposition, sometimes the deposition itself, claiming that the expert's side is responsible for payment.

So, the question arises, how do we as experts keep this from happening? The simplest and most effective way is to have a prepared document for payment. Simply stated, your fee schedule should outline your hourly rate, delineation for preparation, analysis, travel, lodging, meals, reports, and testimony with signature agreements by you and the attorney. Ethical standards dictate that this portion of your services be clearly outlined and defined.

Once the deposition is taken, the expert witness has a chance to review the deposition and make any changes within 30 days after being notified that the transcript is available. If changes are made, the deponent expert is to sign and list the changes. It is also possible that the deposition is taken by written questions. There are advantages and disadvantages to either a written or oral deposition. Let us look at each separately.

Written Depositions. At first thought it may appear that this type of deposition is the least intrusive and difficult because all that is required is to answer the question. Smart attorneys can easily set a trap in the question they ask. In many instances, a follow-up question may more clearly define the interrogatory. Simply answering the question may not explain the nuances in the question. The written question may also not reveal the intent and the body language of the questioner which might reveal the true intent of the question. Written answers also do not necessarily reveal the veracity and experience of the expert in their testimony. The demeanor of the expert is sometimes crucial when the jury takes up the case. This occurs when conditions prevail where the results are left up to the battle of the experts. Which expert is more believable? A true ethical expert is never worried that his veracity will be challenged by his responses. Explaining the facts, evidence, analysis, and calculations with certainty within scientific concepts in a viewable forum should never dissuade the expert.

Oral Depositions. Never hide from the truth. If the expert pursues provable, indisputable science, in the analysis leading up to a conclusion, the truth more often than not emerges. If the truth emerges, notwithstanding the jury verdict, then the expert is ethical. Mainly for these reasons, the preferred method of a deposition should be orally. Keep in mind that a deposition or court testimony is a learned craft. It takes practice to defray the attempts by the opposing attorney to discredit the expert. The simplest and most logical method to address these assaults is to use science and facts. If the expert bends the rules or uses unproven science or simply their experience, the truth will eventually come out.

At a hearing or at trial or a general court proceeding, depositions may be used for a variety of purposes. The deposition may be used in whole or in part against a party based on the following conditions as outlined in Rule 32, Using Depositions in Court Proceedings:

(a) the party was present or represented at the taking of the deposition or had reasonable notice of it;

(b) it is used to the extent it would be admissible under the Federal Rules of Evidence if the deponent were present and testifying; and
(c) the use is allowed by Rule 32.

More specifically, a deposition may be used by a party to impeach or contradict the testimony of the expert as a witness or for any other purpose allowed by the Federal Rules of Evidence. A deposition may be used to introduce the testimony of an expert witness who may be unavailable due to illness, age, infirmity, imprisonment, death, or who is more than 100 miles from the place of the hearing, or on motion and notice there may be exceptional circumstances that allow the deposition to be used instead of live testimony.

If a party offers only a part of a deposition, the adverse party may require that other parts of the deposition be admitted for fairness. A deposition that is lawfully taken in Federal or State Court may be used in a later action involving the same subject matter between the same or different parties. This often creates a conundrum for the expert during testimony. The opposing attorney may dig up an old deposition or testimony where the expert stated some opinion and say, *"did you not say a, b, c in case X?"* You may have said that in a completely different context. Your retort should always be to require them to provide the transcript and to read the entire context of what you said. That strategy always takes the wind out of their sails and reveals their attempt to fictitiously subvert your testimony.

Such a scenario has actually occurred to both of us on more than one occasion. In one instance, the case involved a pedestrian who had been drinking and passed out by a rural road near the road edge after leaving the bar. This event occurred late at night and there was no street lighting. A passing pickup truck failed to see the drunken pedestrian lying on the road and ran over his body causing his death. The question arose whether the driver should have seen the intoxicated, passed out pedestrian. Conspicuity and visibility were the issues at trial. The defense attorney for the driver asked the question: Did you not testify in another case (several years before) that the visibility was different than what you are alleging here? The answer given was: I don't recall but please provide me with the case, deposition, and transcript to refresh my memory. Then I can answer and provide the similarity or difference in the conditions under which I answered that particular question. Of course, the opposing attorney did not have the alleged transcript and simply changed the subject. In other cases, they may ask to read a particular answer in a deposition or testimony transcript that was given which excluded any caveats. In such instances, all you need to do is ask for the preceding or following pages that clarify your answer. The moral here is that if you have been honest, scientific, and ethical, such tricks by the opposition cannot diminish your testimony or impeach you.

THE PAST AND A VIEW OF THE FUTURE

What has happened over the past half of a century or more? In Chapter 9, we wish to outline the most egregious examples of this forensic curse that has affected true science. If you have been reading closely, you will note that we have placed considerable emphasis on the word experience. Experience associated with science is a good thing. What we object to is experience without science. Again, we reiterate that the fields of the forensic sciences must conform to true science and not pseudoscience. Our attempts in this regard are to enlighten the forensic science community with ethical standards for the various practices. We are encouraged by the development in many of the fields of forensics with regulations, standards, and canons of ethics that are being developed in DNA, medical fields, and laboratory sciences where extensive tests, protocols, and experimentation take place. We are more discouraged by the opposition to standards in the fields that we outline in the final chapter. These fields include engineering, tool marks, firearms, electrical arcing, fire char patterns, wind force, gravity, and human injury analysis.

9

Questionable Science and Common Misconceptions

By way of example, we wish to outline some of the most common misconceptions perpetrated by the questionable science that abounds to this day in forensics. In the majority of these fields, there is ample evidence that ethical, scientific principles have not been adhered to. Even though the National Academy of Sciences Report on Forensics has been out for 10 years, significant effort in correcting the problems has not taken place. Inertia is difficult to overcome.

FIRE SCIENCES

Ventilation is a major factor in any fire. A fire is simply the rapid oxidation of the selected material. The rate of burning, or oxidation, is dependent on several factors such as the heat capacity of the material being burned, the ignition source, any accelerant which may have been introduced, the volume of the space where the fire occurs, and the amount of air that is available to aid in the combustion process. The ventilation effect of a fire is seldom analyzed by most fire investigators and is generally disregarded.

On a microscale, the burning process is divided into five separate and distinct stages. These are heating, transition, degradation, decomposition, and oxidation. The investigation of a fire can seldom be broken down into the microscale level where the reactions within a specific polymer are analyzed. Fire sciences deal with the entire material as it burns. Thus, at the macroscale level, the burning process is broken down into another five stages: heating, decomposition, ignition, combustion, and propagation. It is in this last stage, when the fire propagates, aided in large part by ventilation, where many misconceptions in the fire sciences have raised their ugly head.

Char pattern analysis is a common misconception that has been perpetrated because the depth of char is greatly influenced by the ventilating environment. A common misconception is that the depth of char leads to the direction of the fire travel and helps to locate the origin. This may be true in some cases, but cannot be reasonably stated without the influence of the ventilating environment. On the macroscale level, the first four levels of a fire produce ignition and burning with sufficient oxygenation which lead to the propagation stage of a fire. Another method of the selection of the stages of a fire is classified as the initial fire, fire buildup, flashover, fully developed fire, and propagation. In any classification stage of a fire, the effect of ventilation plays a very significant role in the proper assessment of the depth of char on the remaining structures. The reader should note that we are discussing char on wooden members in particular. Wood frame construction is the most widely used method particularly in residential structures in the United States.

There are tools available to study the dynamics of a fire. Over the past 40 years or so, the National Institute of Standards and Technology (NIST), through its Building and Fire Research Laboratory, has developed the Fire Dynamics Simulator (FDS) computer modeling system for the purpose of predicting the transfer of mass and heat as a consequence of a fire. The robustness of the FDS allows the user to introduce "what if" scenarios to aid in the determination of the origin and the progression of the fire. To our knowledge, this is the only scientific tool available to determine any type of char pattern analysis at this point in time.

Without the use of advanced tools such as the FDS in conjunction with extensive weather data to simulate the fire environment, it is ludicrous to attempt to use depth of char to determine the fire progression. Additionally, scaled diagrams, fuel loads, and ventilation effects are seldom considered when most fires are investigated.

In many instances, it is reasonable to perform a simplified analysis of the fire based on observed evidence and some basic accelerant testing. However, in complex events, attempting to apply char patterns and electrical arcing in order to identify the source of the fire can be very misleading and erroneous. We discuss arcing evidence next.

The other area of fire analysis that comes into question is the arcing evidence of electrical conductors. Very often, in many fires, the investigators find multiple areas where electrical wires have arced. Many times, melted conductors are misidentified as revealing arcing. The interpretation of arced conductors may be subject to disagreement because the evidence is always not definitive. If the point of origin can be identified and located at the point of an electrical arc, the arc may have produced the fire. Alternatively, another source may have started the fire at the arced wire location and produced the arcing. Arcing evidence of electrical conductors is easily misidentified for the following reasons. First, copper conductors melt at approximately 1800°F. Aluminum melts at approximately 1200°F. There has always been a misconception that typical fires in residences do not reach the high temperatures necessary to melt copper. This is absolutely incorrect, as detailed in actual fire tests. To further complicate the analysis, it is very difficult in many instances to delineate between melted conductors and short-circuited conductors. Various attempts by many investigators, including the authors, to clearly show definitive proof have been unsuccessful.

Here is what the NAS Report has to say about fires and accelerants: "To assess the effects of an accelerant, one might design an experiment under a range of conditions (e.g., wind speed, temperature, presence/absence of other chemicals) with two groups: one in which materials are burned in the presence of an accelerant ('treatment') and one with no accelerant ('control'). The measured outcomes on the burned materials might be measures that characterize the damage patterns (e.g., depth of char, size of bubbles on surfaces). Differences in the ranges of these measurements from the materials in the two groups (treatment versus control) suggest a hypothesis about the effects of an accelerant. Following this exploration, one should design validation studies to confirm that these measures do indeed characterize the differences in materials treated or untreated with an accelerant." ... "By contrast, much more research is needed on the natural variability of burn patterns and damage characteristics and how they are affected by the presence of various accelerants. Despite the paucity of research, some arson investigators continue to make determinations about whether or not a particular fire was set. However, according to testimony presented to the committee, many of the rules of thumb that are typically assumed to indicate that an accelerant was used (e.g., 'alligatoring' of wood, specific char patterns) have been shown not to be true. Experiments should be designed to put arson investigations on more solid scientific footing."

The authors have conducted fire tests on 13 houses, 2 mobile homes, 4 vehicles, and numerous appliances with temperature instrumentation and video recording. The results of our tests clearly confirm that char pattern analysis and arcing evidence are generally erroneous for the attribution of the fire origin.

ODONTOLOGY

Bite mark comparison is controversial because of some glaring inconsistencies. These are that, as with other areas of the forensic sciences, the uniqueness of human dentition has not been scientifically established. Additionally, the dynamic effect of biting human skin has not been proven to be unique. The distortion of the skin upon biting has not been demonstrated and quantified. It seems reasonable that in some cases bite marks may be used to exclude certain suspects. However, to exclude all other people and limit the dental impression of one human without scientific studies of a large population of individuals is simply unethical. The plasticity of human skin and tissue renders such findings as generally useless.

In summary, the NAS Report concluded the following: "Bite mark testimony has been criticized basically on the same grounds as testimony by questioned document examiners and microscopic hair examiners. The committee received no evidence of an existing scientific basis for identifying an individual to the exclusion of all others." ... "Some research is warranted in order to identify the circumstances within which the methods of forensic odontology can provide probative value."

For many years in the past, and more significantly prior to 1974, dental impressions were used to help identify victims or cadavers by matching dental records. Generally, when these efforts were undertaken, the odontologist was furnished with a complete set of dentition records and a full set of x-rays. When a crime scene is evaluated for the presence of bite marks, glaring problems arise. First, the position of the area receiving the bite is not knowable. For example, assume that a bite impression is deposited on a breast. Several factors will affect the shape of the impression. Was the victim standing, lying on their back, situated on their side, perhaps sitting? Was the arm down, up, to the side, or to an unknown angle? Keep in mind that the breast is mainly composed of adipose tissue which is extremely malleable depending on body position. To further complicate the story, when bite mark impressions are recorded, it is most probable that these recordings are not taken in the same position of the body as when they were deposited. Furthermore, bite mark impressions will not contain a full set of dentitions. Only the biting teeth will generally deposit the marks. Consider for the sake of scientific argument that the biting teeth of two individuals may match but the molar teeth do not. Is this possible? Reason seems to indicate that this may, in fact, be the case.

As Mary A. Bush has shown, a fraction of the available information is deposited from a bite mark impression from a crime. This analysis included a sampling of 500 individuals in which six teeth from the front were found to be indistinguishable in two different people. This analysis shows that all five anatomical surfaces do not create bite marks. Biting results only from the front six teeth generally.

In science, we observe an effect such as a bite mark. We perform tests based on the observation of many such events. We look at the effect of varying parameters in our observations. We analyze the data to determine if our hypothesis is correct. If the tests and their variability do not conform with our hypothesis, then we must modify our hypothesis. In forensic odontology, no such science has been conducted to claim any semblance of validation of bite mark impressions. Bite mark impressions lack the scientific rigor of many forensic fields where the identifier uses their opinion or experience and their bias to make a judgment of a match. Again, the specter of uniqueness raises its ugly head.

FINGERPRINTS

A more descriptive and commonly used term for fingerprint analysis is friction ridge analysis, which is performed on fingers, palms, hands, and feet, and is deemed an individual characteristic. This field of forensics shares similarities with other pattern recognition fields such as shoe impressions, tire marks, tool marks, and handwriting analysis.

According to the NAS Report there is some scientific evidence that friction ridge patterns are unique and persist unchanged throughout the life of an individual. We would agree that this may be the case in a full set of prints, but believe that it is a stretch to extend this conclusion to a partial latent print from a crime scene. As the NAS Report further explains, "uniqueness does not guarantee that prints from two different individuals are sufficiently different that they cannot be confused, or that two impressions made by the same finger will also be sufficiently similar to be discerned as coming from the same source." The NAS Report further states that the impression of a finger differs every time it is taken because of the dynamic uncertainties in the pressure, angle, and rotation of the finger while making the print.

Attempting to quantify the factors that may affect a fingerprint that is deposited are too numerous to define. Some of these factors include body grease or perspiration, blood, oil, paint, food, the surface or substrate, temperature, humidity, direction of the imprint applied, force, callouses, scars, etc. The conditions that lead to the deposition of a fingerprint are never the same and therefore cannot be exactly duplicated. Some of the more notable cases where errors have occurred using fingerprint evidence include the cases of Stephan Cowans, Shirley McKie, Craig Harvey, Rene Sanchez, and, of course, the Brandon Mayfield case in 2004 concerning the Madrid train bombing. Simon Cole, an Irvine, California, criminologist, has found that as many as 1000 incorrect matches could be made each year in the United States by fingerprint analysts. He has pointed out that since proficiency tests beginning in 1983 reveal an error rate of 0.8% multiplied by the large number of cases being analyzed, there may be as many as 1900 mistaken fingerprint analyses each year. To further compound the problem in fingerprint analysis, the Collaborative Testing Service in 1995 administered a proficiency test and of the 156 examiners who took the test, only 68 correctly classified seven latent prints. This alarming rate of error simply cannot be considered science.

Over the past few years, some advancements in fingerprint detection technology have been proposed. These include micro-x-ray fluorescence based on the residue of the chemical elements present in a fingerprint. The National Institute of Standards and Technology has developed a computerized system for the minutia deposited by a fingerprint. Other areas of analysis have also been postulated by a variety of research groups. The American Association for the Advancement of Science has concluded that "There is no basis for estimating the number of individuals who might be the source of a particular latent print. Hence, a latent print examiner has no more basis for concluding that the pool of possible sources is probably limited to a single person than for concluding it is certainly limited to a single person."

TOOL MARKS AND FIREARMS

The alleged scientific field of tool mark identification does not meet the required basic concept associated with science. Tool mark identification is predicated on the unproven and mystical concept that any tool making a mark is unique. For example, if we go to the hardware store and purchase two identical screwdrivers, which were manufactured consecutively, and install them on a jig, which scratches a surface at the same angle, the same length, and the same pressure, will the markings be unique? That is, will the tool mark examiner be able to identify which screwdriver made which scratch? The claim is that it is so. Similarly, it is claimed that the firing pin of a revolver, the ejection mechanism of that gun, or the rifling of the barrel will be unique on the bullet and the casing. Remember that uniqueness requires to the exclusion of all others.

To better understand the dilemma posed by experts in tool marks, we need to review a little history. Before computer-aided machine control was developed circa 1970, machining was performed with lathes, drills, milling machines, grinders, and the like using quite accurate methods that involved many measurements by the machinist. The level of machine accuracy was considered to be five one-thousandths of an inch or 5 mils. A more concise definition of tolerances is considered 0.1 mm or about 0.004 inches which would be 4 mils. In a realistic sense, the machinist would use the lathe, milling machine, or other tool to remove material from the piece that was being manufactured by successively measuring, removing, etc. Between successive cuts of the tool, the machinist would use a set of calipers or dial indicators for the measurement. When the measurements were within the tolerance of 5 mils, the piece would be considered finished.

With the advent of computer numerically controlled (CNC) machines, better accuracy and repeatability were achieved. Today, machines are statistically process controlled (SPC) and can achieve tolerances less than 0.1 mm for very critical components. However, such precision is simply not warranted in applications such as screwdrivers, hammers, wrenches, and firearms.

Within this context, let us see what 5 mils looks like. Figure 9.1 shows a calibration ruler. For comparison, Figure 9.1 shows two lines, one a line width of 0.1 mm or about 0.003937 inches which is 3.937 mils and close to 5 mils. The other line is 0.076 mm. These lines have been magnified 30 times their actual size for comparison. Note that the thinner line is essentially indistinguishable from the 0.1 mm line. Are we to believe that tool mark examiners can distinguish the difference?

The authors conducted some very simple tests in an attempt to prove or disprove the erroneous conclusion that tool marks are unique. Our very simple and limited tests reveal that this is not the case. Consider Figures 9.2 and 9.3 which show two similar High

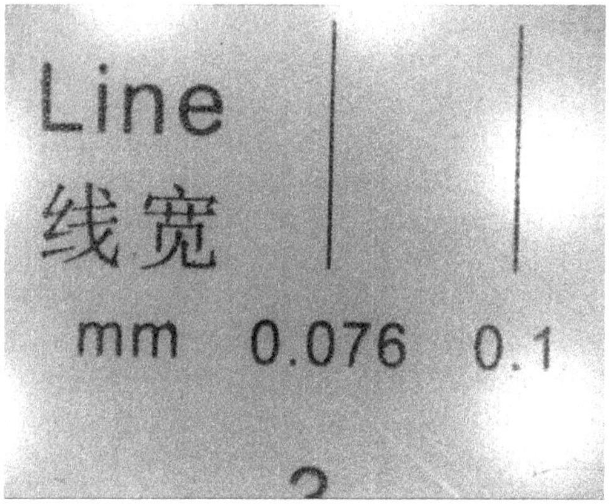

FIGURE 9.1 Line comparison.

Standard pistols. Figure 9.2 is a Target model 2369789 and Figure 9.3 is a Military model 107 2312714.

The uniqueness theory of tool mark examiners states that a tool, such as a gun, will produce identical markings when the firing pin strikes the cartridge. If that is the case, why does Figure 9.4 show two subsequent firing pin impressions from the same High Standard Target model differ? Figure 9.5 also shows dissimilar firing pin marks on a different cartridge fired from the High Standard Military model.

FIGURE 9.2 Target model pistol.

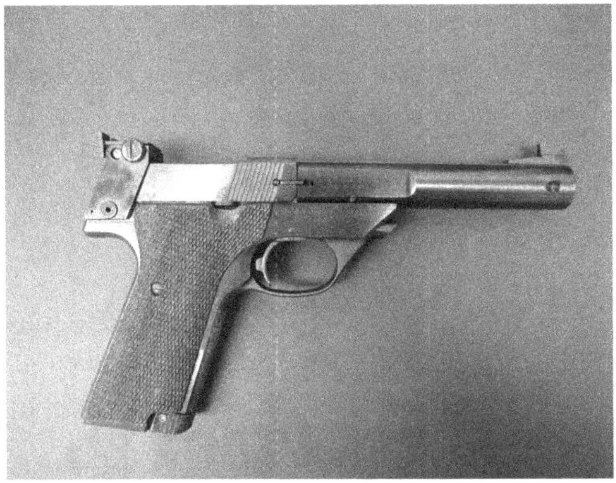

FIGURE 9.3 Military model pistol.

Let us now look at the lands and grooves produced by these two automatic revolvers.

Can you tell which lands and grooves were created by which gun? Were they all created by the same gun? Were they all created by the two different guns? Actually, in Figure 9.6 the markings were created by the different guns and those in Figure 9.7 were created by the same gun. These are simply the most noticeable examples that the authors produced from firing 34 rounds of ammunition, 18 rounds from the Target model and 16 from the Military model. Yes,

FIGURE 9.4 Subsequent cartridge marks from the Target model pistol.

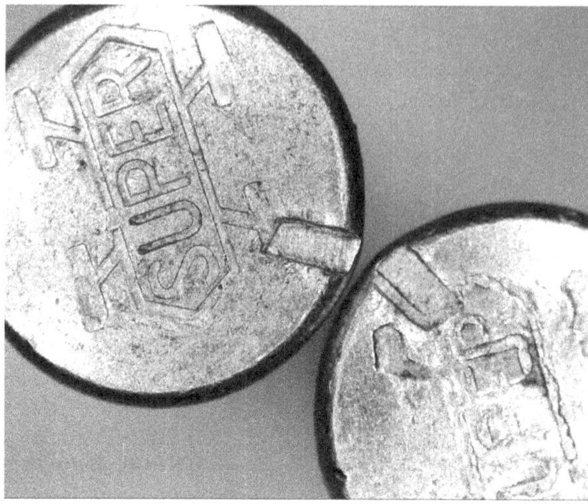

FIGURE 9.5 Subsequent cartridge marks from the Military model pistol.

some of the patterns produced could be noted as being produced from the same gun. However, many have too many distinct markings which would lead to erroneous results.

One argument we have heard is that using 22 caliber ammunition may yield inconclusive results. How can this be true if the claim is that all tool marks are unique? Maybe there are more significant differences with smaller calibers, maybe not. Where is the science

FIGURE 9.6 Lands and grooves from different pistols.

FIGURE 9.7 Lands and grooves from the Target pistol.

that quantifies the discrepancies that may arise? Let us take just a very simple analysis of what we have shown. Consider Figure 9.8.

The question asked in Figure 9.8 is if all the shell casings were fired from the same pistol? We will not reveal the answer but use the diagram in Figure 9.8 to suggest a method of analysis for comparison. In this diagram, all the line widths are 0.1 mm. Note that the ejection pin line for all three casings has been aligned with respect to the reference centers. However, the firing pin lines do not align and neither do the alignment circles. This type of analysis could be used to produce scientifically more significant determinations with respect to tool mark identification. The clear indication from our limited tests simply disproves the assertion that tool marks are unique and reproducible. To assert otherwise is simply not scientific or ethical. To our knowledge, no scientific methodology exists for tool mark analysis.

STRUCTURES, GRAVITY, AND WIND

Probably the most recent example of ethical failures in construction and engineering is the Florida International University bridge collapse in Miami, Florida. This bridge design was essentially a post-tension concrete structure with an unsymmetrical design to accommodate the traffic lanes of US 41 that ran east and west under the bridge. Soon after the main structure was placed atop its piers, inspectors noted cracks developing near one of the diagonal members. These cracks continued to propagate and widen as time

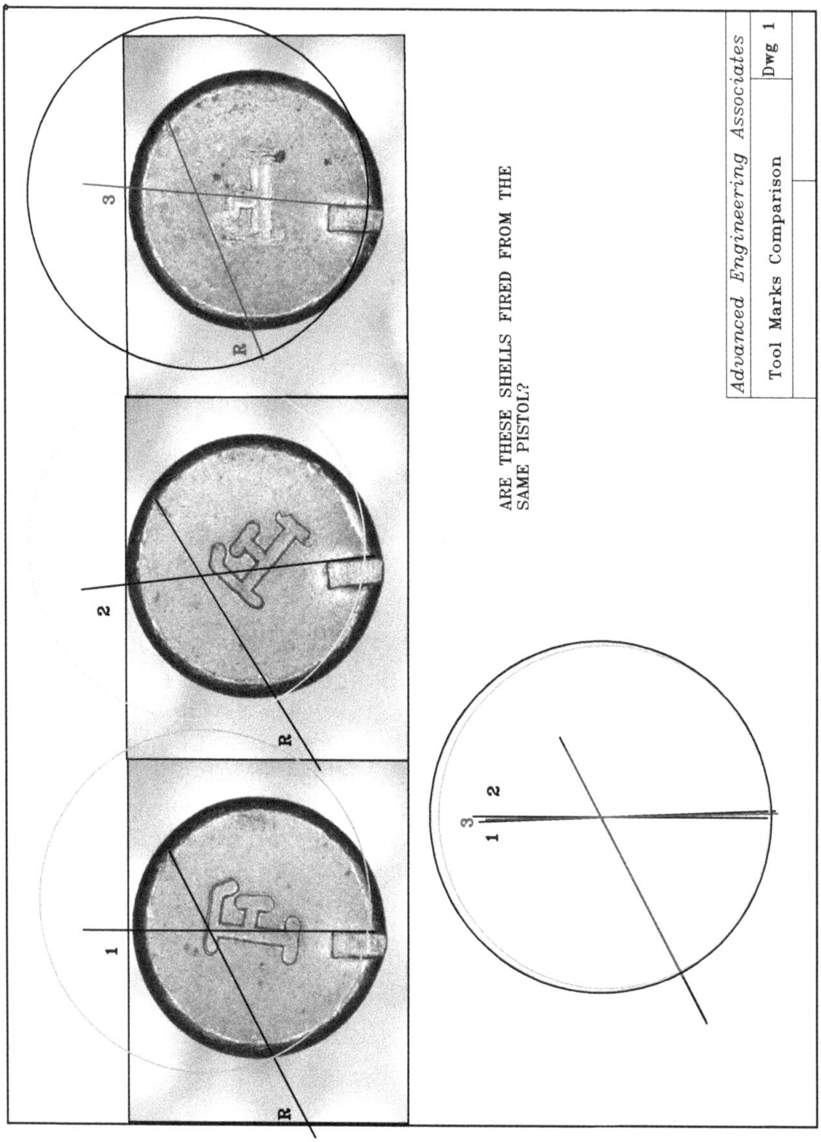

FIGURE 9.8 Possible analysis to compare tool marks.

passed. On the morning of the bridge collapse, at a meeting, the engineer of record had assured the team members of the project that the structure was not at risk. In retrospect, this assurance by the engineer of record is a flagrant lapse in ethical behavior and by the time that the meeting took place it was simply too late to take corrective action. Developing and widening cracks in pre-stressed

FIGURE 9.9 Florida International University bridge collapse.

concrete are most certainly indicative of failure. Figure 9.9 taken from news accounts shows the collapsed pedestrian bridge.

Fortunately, the collapse killed and injured only a handful of people. A much more catastrophic collapse occurred in the Kansas City Hyatt Regency walkway in 1981. This collapse, produced by improper changes in the structural design of the walkways, was the deadliest collapse produced by structural design malfeasance in the United States. The collapse killed 114 people and injured 216. The atrium rose four levels and consisted of walkways on the second and fourth floors directly above each other. The third-floor walkway was offset toward the interior of the atrium and was not affected. The fourth-floor walkway collapsed onto the second floor and the entire structure collapsed to the main floor of the atrium. The walkways were suspended from hanger rods 1.25 inches in diameter.

As a result of constructability issues, the original design was modified by the architect and the steel fabricator but was not approved via calculations by the engineering team. The design change was simply approved by the engineer over the phone without providing an engineering analysis. Figure 9.10 shows the modification made in order to ease the constructability issues that arose.

In typical engineering courses consisting of strength requirements for structural integrity, a safety factor is always considered. This safety factor varies generally from a value of 1.5 to 2.0. That is, if they are required to support a load of say 1000 pounds, the structural members in question should be designed to support between

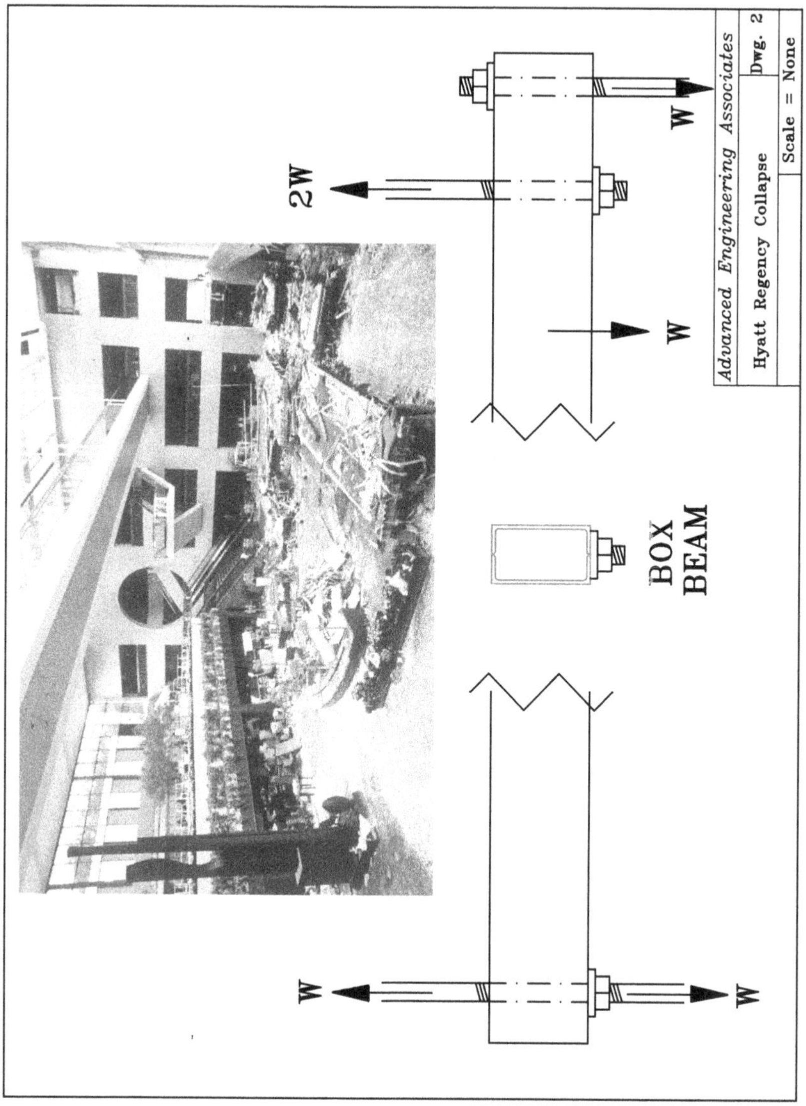

FIGURE 9.10 Kansas City Hyatt Regency walkway collapse.

1500 and 2000 pounds. As we can see in Figure 9.10, the actual construction produced a reaction on the supporting rod of twice the load which is at the limit of safety design and was responsible for the failure. This collapse in the Hyatt is a classic model of the non-adherence to engineering ethics. The alternative design should never have been approved without proper engineering structural calculations.

This last example is one of the most egregious we have encountered as forensic engineers. Let us set up the case: A house sits on a steep hillside and is subjected to significant hydraulic forces. Common with substandard construction, the footings, basement walls, and perimeter drain systems are insufficient to carry the loads imposed by water flow, hydrostatic forces, and gravity. As a result of this substandard construction, the foundation wall against the hillside bows inward. It is evident that this failure process has been occurring over an extended period of time. Not days, weeks, or months, but the failure has been progressing for years and began right after the house was constructed. The wall failure is well documented and a claim was previously submitted to the insurance company. The insurance company denied the claim because such an event was not covered under the policy. A couple of years later, a wind storm passed through the area with gusts in the 30–40 mile per hour range. The wind gusts are verified by the National Weather Service to peak at 35 miles per hour.

Through his attorney, the insured hired a forensic engineer who stated the following. "The wind caused the foundation to shift from the house producing the offset visible in the foundation wall." That type of discrepancy is often seen after a hurricane or tornado occurs in flat terrain but not in the area where the house was situated in steep hilly terrain in the Appalachian Mountains. What is observed is the house shifting from the foundations before there is any movement of the foundations, not the reverse as claimed in this case. Also note that hurricanes and tornadoes reach wind speeds in the 100–200 mile range when they affect structures.

This ludicrous claim by the alleged expert is used to submit another claim to repair the foundations resulting from wind damage. Is such a scenario possible? Notwithstanding the previous claim which was well documented and investigated, it is a simple proposition to disprove this new claim. The values we use in the example are typical for a one-story house.

Wind pressure is determined from

$$P = 0.00256V^2$$

where

P = wind pressure in lb/sf

V = wind speed in mph

For a flat surface such as the side of a building, the drag coefficient, A_d, varies from 1.4 to 2.0. Two other considerations are the exposure coefficient, K_z, and the gust response, G_h. Where

$$K_z = \left[\frac{z}{33}\right]^{\left[\frac{2}{7}\right]}, \ z = \text{height at midpoint}$$

$$G_h = 0.65 + 0.6\left[\frac{h}{33}\right]^{\left[\frac{1}{7}\right]}, \ h = \text{height of exposed area}$$

the wind pressure equation then becomes

$$P = 0.00256 A_d K_z G_h V^2$$

For a wall area of 320 sf, $z = 11$, $A_d = 2.0$, $K_z = 0.73058$, $G_h = 1.16$, and $V = 35$ mph, the pressure is

$$P = 5.31 \text{ \#/sf}$$

so that the total force is 1700 pounds, which is insufficient to move the house. More importantly, the claim was that the house did not move but the foundations actually moved and the house remained in place. For those calculations, the foundations exposure is as follows:

Foundation area = 120 sf, $z = 1.5$, $A_d = 2.0$, $K_z = 0.413$, $G_h = 1.075$, and the pressure is

$$P = 2.78 \text{ \#/sf}$$

then the total force is 333 pounds. Now consider the number of blocks that make up the exposed foundations. The height of the exposed block is 3 feet or 4.5 blocks and the length is 30 blocks for 40 feet. So, the total number of blocks that would be moved in such a ridiculous event would be 135 blocks. Considering just gravity, ignoring the weight of the house, another preposterous assumption, a coefficient of friction of 0.5, the weight of each block would have to be about 5 pounds. Surprise, 8 inch blocks weigh more than 5 pounds. Also, the coefficient of friction would actually be greater than 1.

Of course, the opposing expert did not do some simple calculations as we have outlined and ignored prior evidence that hydrostatic pressure on the foundation wall caused the distress. Such work and opinions are without foundation and unethical.

Appendix A: Values of Fundamental Constants

Quantity	Symbol	Value
Acceleration due to gravity	g	9.806 m/s^2
Atomic mass	M_a	1.66×10^{-27} Kg
Avogadro's constant	N_0	6.022×10^{23} molecules/mol
Boltzmann's constant	k	1.38×10^{-23} Joule/°K
Conductance quantum	G_o	7.748×10^{-5} Siemens
Electric constant	E_o	8.854×10^{-12} Farads/m
Electron mass	m_e	9.109×10^{-31} Kg
Electron volt	eV	1.602×10^{-19} Joules
Electron charge	q_e	-1.602×10^{-19} Coulomb
Faraday constant	F	9.6485×10^{4} Coulomb/mol
Fine structure constant	α	7.297×10^{-3}
Magnetic constant	μ_0	$4\pi \times 10^{-7}$ N/A^2
Magnetic flux quantum	Φ_0	2.067×10^{-15} Webbers
Molar gas constant	R_0	8.314 Joule/(mol-°K)
Molar mass constant	M_μ	10^{-3} Kg/mol
Newtonian gravitational constant	G	6.673×10^{-11} $m^3/(Kg\text{-}s^2)$
Planck's constant	h	6.625×10^{-23} Joule-s
Proton mass	m_p	1.672×10^{-27} Kg
Speed of light in a vacuum	C_0	2.9979×10^{8} m/s
Stefan-Boltzmann constant	σ	5.67×10^{-8} $W/(m^2\text{-}K^4)$
Standard atmosphere	1 atm	1.013×10^{5} Pa (N/m^2)
Standard state pressure	ssp	10^{5} Pa
Zero temperature	°K	–273.15 °C

Appendix B: Conversion Factors

Length

1 in = 2.54 cm
1 ft = 30.48 cm

Area

1 cm^2 = 0.155 in^2
1 m^2 = 10.76 ft^2

Volume

1 ft^3 = 0.0283 m^3
1 L = 1000 cm^3 = 0.2462 gal
1 in^3 = 16.39 cm^3 = 4.329×10^{-3} gal

Velocity

1 ft/s = 0.6818 mph

Acceleration

1 m/s^2 = 3.281 ft/s^2

Force

1 lb = 4.448 N = 4.448×10^5 dynes = 0.4535 Kg

Mass

1 g = 6.85×10^{-5} slug = 10^{-3} Kg
1 slug = 32.17 lb

Pressure

1 atm = 14.7 psi = 1.013×10^6 dynes/cm^2 = 29.92 in Mercury @ 0°C
Pa = N/m^2

Energy

1 J = 10^7 ergs = 0.239 cal = 9.48×10^{-4} Btu = 0.7376 ft-lb = 2.778 $\times 10^{-4}$ W-h
1 N-m = 0.7376 ft-lb
1 erg = 7.367×10^{-8} ft-lb

EXPLANATION OF ABBREVIATIONS

in: inches
ft: feet
cm: centimeters
m: meters
L: liters
gal: gallons
mph: miles per hour
lb: pounds
s: seconds
Kg: kilograms
N: Newtons
atm: atmospheres
J: Joules
cal: calories
Btu: British thermal units
W: Watts
h: hours
Pa: Pascals
g: gram

Bibliography

Adebisi, Samuel (2008) Fingerprint Studies—The Recent Challenges and Advancements. A Literary Review. *The Internet Journal of Biological Anthropology*, vol. 2, no. 2.

Alder, Ken (2007) *The Lie Detectors*. New York: Free Press. ISBN 0-7432-5988-2.

American Association for the Advancement of Science (February 25, 2019) Anne Q. Hoy, 15, Sep. 2017.

Ashbaugh, David R. (1999) *Qualitative Friction Ridge Analysis: An Introduction to Basic and Advanced Ridgeology*. Boca Raton, FL: CRC Press.

Ballard, Robert D. & Dunmore, Spencer (1995) *Exploring the Lusitania*. New York: Warner Books.

Basham, Arthur Llewellyn (1981) *History and Doctrines of the Ajivikas—A Vanished Indian Religion*. New Delhi: Motilal Banarsidass. ISBN 978-81-208-1204-8.

Beesly, Patrick (1982) *Room 40: British Naval Intelligence, 1914–1918*. Long Acre, London: Hamish Hamilton Ltd. ISBN 0-241-10864-0.

Booth, Martin (2000) *The Doctor and the Detective: A Biography of Sir Arthur Conan Doyle*. New York: Minotaur Books.

Boyer, Carl B. (1991) *A History of Mathematics*, 2nd Edition. New York: Wiley. ISBN 0-471-54397-7.

Bruno, Leonard C. (1989) *The Landmarks of Science*. New York: Facts On File. ISBN 0-8160-2137-6.

Bush, Mary A., Bush, Peter, & Sheets, David H. (2011) Statistical Evidence for the Similarity of Human Dentition. *Journal of Forensic Sciences*, vol. 56, no. 1, pp. 118–123.

Clarke, Desmond (2006) *Descartes: A Biography*. Cambridge: Cambridge University Press. ISBN 0-521-36696-8.

Cooke, Bill (2006) *Dictionary of Atheism, Skepticism, and Humanism*. Amherst, NY: Prometheus Books. ISBN 978-1-59102-299-2.

Farrington, Benjamin (1951) *Francis Bacon, Philosopher of Industrial Science*. New York: Henry Schuman. ISBN 978-0-374-92706-6.

Federal Rules of Evidence (December 1, 2014). Washington, DC: US Publishing Office.

*Federal Rules of Evidence (*2018 *Edition)*. Grand Rapids, MI: Michigan Legal Publishing Ltd. ISBN-13: 978-1-64002-021-4, ISBN-10: 1-64002-021-7.

*Federal Rules of Civil Procedure (*2018 *Edition)*. Grand Rapids, MI: Michigan Legal Publishing Ltd. ISBN-13: 978-1-64002-019-1, ISBN-10: 1-64002-019-5.

*Federal Rules of Criminal Procedure (*2018 *Edition)*. Grand Rapids, MI: Michigan Legal Publishing Ltd. ISBN-13: 978-1-64002-022-1, ISBN-10: 1-64002-022-5.

Feynman, Richard (1965) *The Character of Physical Law*. Cambridge: MIT Press. ISBN 0-262-56003-8.

Guth, Alan H. (1998) *The Inflationary Universe. The Quest for a New Theory of Cosmic Origins.* New York: Basic Books. ISBN 978-0201328400.

Hamilton, Charles (1991) *The Hitler Diaries.* Lexington, KY: The University Press of Kentucky. ISBN 978-0-8131-1779-3.

Hawking, Stephen, J. (2011) *The Dreams That Stuff Is Made Of.* Philadelphia, PA: Running Press. ISBN 978-0-7624-3434-3.

Hueske, Edward (2009) *Firearms and Fingerprints.* New York: Facts On File/Infobase Publishing. ISBN 978-0-8160-5512-8.

Internet Encyclopedia of Philosophy. Ethics (http://www.iep.utm.edu/ethics).

Kuhn, Thomas S. (1962) *The Structure of Scientific Revolutions,* 2nd Edition 1970, 3rd Edition 1996. Chicago, IL: University of Chicago Press.

Marshall, R.D., Pfrang, E.O., Leyendecker, E.V., Woodward, K.A., Reed, R.P., Kasen, M.B., & Shives, T.R. (1982) *Investigation of the Kansas City Hyatt Regency Walkway Collapse.* Washington, DC: US Department of Commerce, National Bureau of Standards.

McClellan, James (1989) *The Common Law Tradition - Liberty, Order, and Justice: An Introduction to the Constitutional Principles of American Government.* Liberty Fund.

Miller, Russell (2008) *The Adventures of Arthur Conan Doyle: A Biography.* New York: Thomas Dunne Books.

Moseley, Alexander (2007) *John Locke: A Continuum Library of Educational Thought.* London: Continuum International Publishing Group. ISBN 0-8264-8405-0.

National Academy of Sciences (2002) *The Polygraph and Lie Detection.* Washington, DC: National Academy Press.

National Research Council (2009) *Strengthening Forensic Sciences in the United States. A Path Forward.* Washington, DC: National Academics Press. ISBN: 0-309-13131-6.

Pankanti, Sharath, Prabhakar, Salil, & Jain, Anil K. (2002) On the Individuality of Fingerprints. *IEEE Transactions on Pattern Analysis and Machine Intelligence,* vol. 24, no. 8, pp. 1010–1025.

Paul, Richard & Elder, Linda (2006) *The Miniature Guide to Understanding the Foundations of Ethical Reasoning.* New York: Foundation for Critical Thinking Free Press. ISBN 0-944583-17-2.

President's Council of Advisors on Science and Technology (PCAST) (2016) Washington, DC.

Rudman, Peter (2007) *How Mathematics Happened. The First 50,000 Years.* New York: Prometheus Books. ISBN 978-1-59102-477-4.

Smith, Kurt (2010) *Matter Matters: Metaphysics and Methodology in the Early Modern Period.* Oxford: Oxford University Press.

Sullivan, John (2007) *Gatekeeper.* Dulles, VI: Potomac Books Inc. ISBN 1-59797-045-X.

Williams, Robert C. (2015) *The Forensic Historian: Using Science to Reexamine the Past.* Abingdon: Routledge. ISBN 978-1-317-45680-3.

Index